DENNIS HOPPER

DENNIS HOPPER

A Madness to His Method

ELENA RODRIGUEZ

A 2M COMMUNICATIONS LTD. PRODUCTION

St. Martin's Press
New York

DENNIS HOPPER: A MADNESS TO HIS METHOD.

Design by Claudia Carlson

Library of Congress Cataloging-in-Publication Data

Rodriguez, Elena.
    Dennis Hopper, a madness to his method.

    "A Thomas Dunne Book."
        1. Hopper, Dennis, 1936–   2. Motion picture
actors and actresses—United States—Biography.
3. Motion picture producers and directors—United States
—Biography.   I. Title.
PN2287.H66R64   1988   791.43′028′0924   [B]   88-11656
ISBN 0-312-02190-9

First Edition

10 9 8 7 6 5 4 3 2 1

DENNIS HOPPER

CHAPTER ONE

To Dennis Hopper, the long sunny days of his boyhood on a Kansas farm were never without drama. As a skinny kid with wistful eyes, his mind constructed his first theater on earth's bare stage. Unsuspecting cows and chickens were the other actors pressed into service by the youthful director. They watched curiously as young Dennis picked up a scrap of wooden fence and turned instantly into Errol Flynn—defending his ship from pirates swarming up the sides. Another day his BB gun became a high-powered rifle and nine-year-old Dennis, hunkering down in a haystack, zeroed in on black and white cows that to him became advancing Nazi hordes. And when he stared into the distance, it was not the flat lands of Kansas that he saw. His mind's eye discerned the mountain ranges of Tibet, the skyscrapers of Manhattan, the quietly flowing Danube, all easily reached on the magic carpet of his imagination.

But when they called him home from his travels for supper, reality was Grandmother Davis's farm where Dennis was born May 17, 1936, a few miles from Dodge City. Grandfather and Grandmother Davis were his mother's parents. They were also Dennis's best friends. As a child he felt let down by his mom and dad, he later said, because they did not share the interest in him or give the love that his grandparents provided. His mother, Marjorie Hopper, worked in Dodge City, where she managed a swimming pool and gave lessons. Dennis was always thrilled on the rare occasions she took him into town to play at the pool, a double pleasure because he spent time with her all day and exercised his fertile imagination as a diver and shark hunter.

Dennis's father, Jay Hopper, was also a distant figure, away most of the time because of his job as a traveling postal worker on the railroad. Dennis was five when his mother took him aside soon after the start of World War II, imparting the sad news that his father had been killed in a munitions accident during basic training. The little boy was too young to appreciate the full impact of this news, but he took comfort in her assurances that he would "meet Daddy again in heaven."

The farm where Dennis spent most of his formative years was twelve acres of peace and security, where he had the run of the place. All around were endless wheat fields, a fantastic flat horizon with incredible electric storms, sunsets like the northern lights. He spent most of his time with Grandmother Davis because Grandpa often worked sixty miles away on a big wheat farm near Garden City. It was a lonely life for Dennis, who had few friends, but it spawned the need to fantasize, and from fantasies he would make his future living. His grandparents never challenged the strange sight of a small boy fighting off imaginary armies on a distant haystack. They knew and understood Dennis's wild imagination, even wondering aloud on occasion whether the boy was a budding actor. His interest in drama had been sparked when he was about six, a gift from his grandmother, when she introduced him to the magical world of movies.

The first time, Dennis was outside playing when his grandmother called him. "Help me gather up these eggs," she said, "and I'll have a special treat for you." Dennis happily helped her collect the eggs, which she carried to town in her apron. Dennis trotted along beside her as she went from house to house selling the eggs. With the egg money, she bought their movie tickets. It became a weekly adventure that Dennis looked forward to and learned from. The movies provided rich inspiration for his cast of imaginary characters and for new adventures in "strange lands" around the farm.

"Every Saturday, my grandmother took me to the movies in Dodge City," he later recalled. "We'd go to the Crown or the Dodge—dingy little theaters with balconies. I saw them all—Roy Rogers, Gene Autry, Smiley Burnette, Wild Bill Elliott, occasionally a Randolph Scott war picture. Then all the next week I'd live that picture. If it was a war picture, I'd dig foxholes; if it was sword fighting, I'd poke the cows with a stick. Those dark little Kansas theaters, Saturday afternoons, man, that was big news to me. The old cliché, dig? Like Thomas Wolfe wanting to see where the trains were going to. I wanted to see where those movies were coming from."

Real life proved as amazing as the movies when Dennis's father came back from the dead as the war ended. His death had been an elaborate cover-up because his father had been working in top-secret intelligence.

Dennis recalled later: "My mother was the only one who knew that he was alive. I thought he was dead, my grandparents thought he was dead, everybody thought he was dead. But my father was actually in China, Burma, and India. He was fighting with Mao, he took the surrender from the Japanese in Peking."

The youngster welcomed his father back with wide eyes;

3

he was not somebody who had died in a mundane training accident, he was a real-life hero who had worked as an American spy! Dennis was thrilled, fascinated, and proud of his dad, especially as Jay Hopper had not made much of an earlier impression on his son.

His father returned to his job on the railways, again becoming a distant figure for the youngster who remained on the farm. His mother had yet another job in Dodge City that kept her away.

As glad as he was that his father was alive, the thought that his mother had lied to him sat uneasily on Dennis's psyche; it was a betrayal. She explained that she had been sworn to top secrecy, had been told to live as a widow. But it was an early lesson to Dennis that even adults could not be completely relied upon, were not totally trustworthy. Maybe it was better to live a fantasy life—at least then you knew it was all fake.

Although Dennis was not exactly unhappy and never complained, the lack of a full life with his parents disturbed him.

But his grandparents were shocked when his curiosity and quest for new sensations took a bizarre turn. Dennis found out that if he sniffed enough gasoline from the tank of his grandfather's truck, he would begin to hallucinate and the sky would fill with clowns and goblins, all manner of fanciful creatures taking shape in the clouds. One day he sniffed more than enough gasoline, enough to send him into a violent frenzy. He took up a baseball bat and broke the windshield and the headlights on the truck. There was hell to pay for that. And worse, no more movies with his grandmother until she was sure he had learned his lesson. He gave up sniffing gasoline, but the idea of altering his consciousness had been planted and the experience enjoyed. Soon he would be sneaking beers from the refrigerator and hiding out in the tall wheat while he drank them.

4

When Grandfather Davis was there, Dennis would follow him around, watching him work, gleaning all sorts of valuable information about the land, the farm, and its animals. As Dennis got bigger and stronger, Grandfather Davis dragged him off of his imaginary stage to help around the farm. Instead of seeing distant lands, contemplating the perfumes of Arabia, Dennis mucked out the pigsty and cleaned out the chicken run.

Grandmother Davis put Dennis to work in her Victory Garden weeding and hoeing. In return for his labors, his grandmother would make him wonderful raw onion sandwiches. Dennis would take his sandwich and sit out between rows of tomatoes, thinking about the cycle of nature that was all around him on the farm, soaking up the late-summer sunshine, wondering about his future.

It came as a shock to Dennis when his mother arrived to collect him from his grandparents' and to tell him that he would be joining his parents in a move to Kansas City, Missouri. Marjorie Hopper, always anxious for more material success, thought they could have a better life in a bigger town. By this time Dennis had a little brother, David, six years his junior, who was getting most of his parents' attention. Dennis hated being away from the farm and his grandparents, but he adjusted. As a young kid he started picking up spending money by racking balls in a pool hall. Although not quite in his teens yet, he was hanging out with older boys, smoking cigarettes, drinking beer with the guys when the group managed to get some. He liked the way the beer changed his head—a bit like the gasoline sniffing, but not as out of control. It gave him the confidence to be a tough guy, like the movie gangsters.

His parents worried terribly about Dennis; he seemed remote to them and his overactive imagination appeared to be dominating him. The company he kept was a bad influence. His mother wanted him to apply himself more at school. She had big plans for Dennis; she wanted him to become a doctor or a lawyer, a respectable and useful member of society. But Dennis was not interested in school, the learning by rote, the dreary teachers. He managed to show some enthusiasm for drama, art, and history. His mother and father thought he was rebellious but that they could discipline him back into scholarship. It did not work. When they kept him home, Dennis drifted off into his own world, a place where he could always retreat in order to act out his myriad fantasies. When his parents insisted he sit with his books doing his homework, the only result at the end of an evening was a few pictures he had drawn. His parents could not keep him home indefinitely, and when he got out it was back to the boys at the pool hall. When he came home smelling of beer and tobacco smoke, his mother would burst into tears and his father would tell him he was no good.

Then his parents got a break. Dennis found art, settling into art classes at the Nelson Art Gallery in Kansas City, where the teacher said he actually had real talent. Even though it was an excellent outlet for his creative energy, it did not stop him from sneaking off to the pool hall, drinking beer, and puffing cigarettes.

CHAPTER TWO

If Dennis's parents had not decided to move to California in 1950, it would have been a huge setback to his eventual career. It was in California where he really came into his own, where he learned that the rich imagination he had cultivated on the farm was his ticket to fame and fortune. The family moved west because of his little brother's asthma condition. As David's attacks had gotten worse and more frequent, doctors recommended a change to the milder climate and ocean air of California.

Jay and Marjorie Hopper were anxious to do whatever they could to improve little David's health. Besides, Mrs. Hopper's ambition demanded better opportunities for her family. There were more jobs on the coast, the sun always shone, and the schools offered her boys wider academic choices than those in Kansas City.

Before they moved, Dennis had looked at the map and had seen that San Diego was close to Los Angeles; that meant it was close to Hollywood, where the movies came from. He looked forward to the trip across country, to see the Wild West of his Saturday-matinee adventures, to traverse the great Rocky Mountains. When the family arrived in California, Dennis loved the freeways with gleaming automobiles speeding to magical destinations, or so he imagined. He sat for hours listening to the surf thundering down on the sandy beaches. When he looked across the Pacific, there was another flat horizon line where ocean met sky, just like the one where the Kansas wheat fields ended in the far distance. But the natural beauty did not rate Dennis's unqualified approval.

Later he would say, "I'm creative, man, because of my big disappointment: seeing real mountains and real ocean for the first time. Wow! What a bring-down! The mountains in my head were much bigger than the Rockies . . . the oceans far wider."

Dennis was still not much on studying. The only reading he would do was for a play or a poem he had to memorize. But he was at last happy at the two public schools—two years at Grossmont and his junior and senior years of high school at Helix—he would attend until he was eighteen. Both schools had excellent drama departments, places where he really came alive. He practiced dramatic declamation, reciting poems or soliloquies. He won three dramatic declamation contests in California statewide competitions during his high-school years. He also applied his active imagination to the school debating teams. His parents were proud and surprised at the changes in their boy. But they did not know what it meant when Dennis seemed on another planet and the pupils of his eyes were dilated. Dennis was now puffing weed as well as cigarettes, quenching the marijuana-induced thirst with bottles of beer. Like most of the other kids, he loved to party. And they all roared with laughter when Dennis was high: He was outrageously funny, mimicking teachers, telling jokes.

Dennis's introduction to the real entertainment world came when he won a spot on an Art Linkletter talent show. He received an ovation for reciting Vachel Lindsay's poem "Abraham Lincoln Walks at Midnight." The acclaim was addictive. He wanted more of that, and now he knew how he could get it.

There was real theater in San Diego—the Old Globe where they even did Shakespeare's plays, and up the road a bit, in the town of La Jolla, was the La Jolla Playhouse. Dennis loved the smell and atmosphere of these places, spending precious pocket money, earned delivering newspapers and collecting old bottles, to buy his admission. It was at the Old Globe that he made his acting debut, playing an urchin in a production of Charles Dickens's *A Christmas Carol*. He easily won the audition, effortlessly reading a portion of the script with all the dramatic emphases in the right places. That short Christmastime run only whetted his appetite for more.

But at home, it was not all sweetness and light. Acting did not conform with his mother's ideas for his future. Sensing her son's proclivity for having a good time, she figured he would wreck his life in the company of other actors and show business people. The arguments with his parents all led to the same admonition: "We don't want you to be an actor, we want you to do something respectable." Inevitably, Dennis would walk away from these conversations, leaving his mom and dad frustrated and furious. Their pride in his earlier successes melted when they thought he was going to make a career out of the theater.

Years later, Dennis recalled the arguments, saying, "My home life was a nightmare, everybody neurotic because they weren't doing what they wanted to do, and yelling at me when I wanted to be creative, because creative people ended up in bars."

Dennis ignored the parental put-downs. He was not going to live his life to fulfill their dreams, he said, especially as they were both bitter people who had not made their own dreams come true. He was determined to fulfill himself and became involved with the San Diego Community Players Theater in which he started getting small but significant walk-on parts.

Tired of the rows at home, Dennis packed his bags and snuck out of the house early one morning while his mom and dad slept. It was the summer between his sophomore and junior years in high school. He went to Pasadena, a city close to downtown Los Angeles. He had heard there was a theater there, the Pasadena Playhouse. He had also been told it was where a lot of great actors seeking to make their marks on Hollywood had started out and learned their craft.

Arriving in Pasadena, he needed both a job and somewhere to stay. He was nearly broke, with just a few dollars and some loose change jingling in his pants pocket. He took the first minimum-wage job he could find, working as a fry cook in a greasy-spoon café. At the end of his first shift, he called his mom and dad and told them not to worry, but he had to make the break until the end of the summer. They groused and grumbled, but were relieved to hear that he intended to return to school. They didn't like it, but they were exhausted trying to fight their son's theatrical ambitions. Secretly, they hoped Dennis would burn the acting bug out of his system by experiencing a couple of harsh failures.

At the Pasadena Playhouse, nobody paid much attention to Dennis when he presented himself. He was just a sixteen-year-old kid, hanging around, asking a lot of annoying questions about what was going on. No one thought much of his acting experience when he tried to tell them about it. While it was not big time, neither was the Pasadena Playhouse for amateurs.

When Dennis arrived they were preparing for the first play of the summer season. His fervent hope of an acting role fizzled when they told him the only use they had for him was backstage. There Dennis moved props, painted scenery flats, set up lights, and did whatever else they told him. He learned a lot, soaking in the atmosphere and watching every move and gesture, listening to every inflection of speech the actors had to offer. There was no pay for the long hours and hard work—only the reward of watching the building of a play from the ground up.

"It was fabulous, man," he recalled. "I saw it all: from blown lines in the beginning, dress rehearsals, to the final finished production in front of a paying audience. The hairs on my arms bristled when the curtain went up that first night. It was more than enough to make me forget the miseries of flipping burgers at the greasy spoon."

At summer's end, when Dennis had to head back home to once again play at being a typical teenaged high-school junior, he was more than that. He had matured, and instead of being put off from his dream of acting, as his parents had hoped, Dennis had seen what it was really like. He was more determined than ever that it was the actor's life for him.

The summer of 1953, Dennis gave a repeat performance, only this time he got a job closer to home at the La Jolla Playhouse. It was his first real job in theater, though he was paid just enough for room and board. His muscles rippled as he heaved scenery and loaded trucks with theatrical props. And, at last, he was acting and being coached by Dorothy McGuire, who with her husband, photographer John Swope, ran the Playhouse. Other distinguished founders and supporters of the Playhouse included La Jolla native son Gregory Peck and actor-director Mel Ferrer.

Dorothy knew what Dennis was going through. She had debuted on stage at the Omaha Community Playhouse opposite Henry Fonda, at the age of thirteen. She understood Dennis's deep passion for the theater. She told him how, after her debut, she went on to do summer stock, radio soap opera, and Broadway. After that came a career in films.

Dorothy and John became the parents Dennis had always wanted. They watched over him, they saw his talent, and they encouraged him to pursue his goals. He later said he had wished he could swap his real parents for these caring, understanding surrogates. For the first time since his childhood on the farm with his grandparents, Dennis felt at home, accepted and loved.

That summer Dorothy gave Dennis a role in her production of *The Postman Always Rings Twice*. Dennis thought he could never feel happier. The wonderful summer had sped by too quickly. Reluctantly, he went back to San Diego, back to finish his last year of dreary high school. He had made a deep impression on the Swopes; they did not forget their protégé.

Dennis did not learn much that last year of high school; his head was still filled with the theater. To ease the boredom he hung out with the guys, the partying guys—the ones that drove the cool-looking cars. "I was a crazy kid, mixed up with a wild bunch—delinquents, I guess. Thank God I had acting. I could have been stuck with those kids forever."

Girls found Dennis fascinating, with an odd mixture of attraction and fear of his wild side. He was handsome and mature, but his personality could be too intense. He was a fun guy around his buddies, but when he became serious about his "work," it was hard for teenage girls to understand. His ambitions ran far higher than those of his peers. His wide-ranging imagination left them behind. They were so impressed with his drive and ambition, they voted him "most likely to succeed."

Dennis didn't care what other kids thought of him. He had his eye on the future. Through contacts at the Old Globe Theater in San Diego, he heard of an acting scholarship to the National Shakespeare Festival at the Globe. He won against stiff competition from nearly three hundred other applicants. It meant a summer of spear-carrying and playing minuscule roles.

That summer at the Old Globe, Dennis became a real actor. He played Montano in *Othello*, was Sebastian in *Twelfth Night*, and Lorenzo in *The Merchant of Venice*. He mastered the challenging rhythms of Shakespearean English. He put real life into the parts. Dorothy McGuire and John Swope came to the Old Globe to see him perform and were pleased to see their confidence in him was justified. That first summer with them had not been a fluke—young Hopper had real talent, the spark that made people watch and listen when he was onstage.

Dorothy advised Dennis that when his scholarship ended, the next step had to be Hollywood or New York. She said she had contacts in Hollywood who would be willing to help in developing his career. So at eighteen he was on his way to the big time.

CHAPTER THREE

Hollywood was just a three-hour freeway hop from San Diego, but Dennis felt that he had landed in another world—a vicious, backbiting town full of greedy people who jealously guarded their domain from newcomers, a place that ate up talent and shattered the dreams of actors and actresses who more often than not went running back to the safety of their hometowns. But Dennis would turn out to be one of the lucky ones, getting important breaks within weeks of coming to town. And he had the talent to back up his luck.

When he arrived in Los Angeles in November 1954, he followed up on the list of contacts supplied by his loyal friend Dorothy McGuire. He went to see Ruth Burch, a casting director at Hal Roach Studios, who provided a tiny walk-on bit in a television series, *Cavalcade of America*.

That brief appearance was enough to interest an agent in handling his fledgling career. His appearance on *Cavalcade* was followed by a ten-line role in another series that led to a big break: a successful audition for a juicy part in the television series *Medic.*

Dennis was reading for the character of an epileptic and the director viewed the healthy young man before him skeptically. He had already seen a lot of young Hollywood hopefuls; there were thirty-two others vying for the part, some of them with far more television experience than Dennis. He did some line readings from the scene, and at the end the director asked him if he thought he could portray an epileptic fit. The next thing the man knew, Dennis was having one right before his eyes. He was gripped by convulsions and his eyes rolled up in his head. Momentarily the director was so convinced, he thought the idiot casting agent had sent him a real epileptic. As suddenly as he had started, Dennis stopped his convulsions. He looked to the director for approval, and the man just shook his head in wonder and said, "We'll let you know, kid."

That afternoon the word came: Dennis had the part in the episode called "Boy in the Storm." It was the kind of featured role that couldn't be missed like those quick walk-ons. He had to be good in this. It was his biggest part so far, and *Medic* was a popular show that lots of people watched, including talent scouts for the big movie studios. They scanned television shows constantly for fresh young talent.

Dennis gave the part everything, winning praise from the producers. Looking back later, he remembered, "They said my seizure was the best they'd seen, indistinguishable from the real thing." The only disappointment was that it would not be aired for months. He had to find a way to live until then.

Things had happened quickly for the Hollywood newcomer, but his money went just as quickly and the television roles seemed few and far between. Nobody had yet seen "Boy in the Storm." The three hundred dollars he was paid for the

Medic episode ran out quickly. Dennis survived doing any odd jobs he could pick up. When there were no odd jobs or bit parts and he was broke, he recalled, he even stole the milk and orange juice delivered to the porches of nearby homes. Like many before him, hunger forced him back home to survive.

"Around Christmas time I took a job for the telephone company delivering phone books," he said. "It was pretty funny. I would ring the bell and hand someone a telephone book and they would ask, 'Didn't I see you on *Cavalcade of America?*'"

In San Diego, Dennis also had to endure the jeering of former school pals who wanted to know why the big-deal movie star was back home taking menial temporary work. They rejoiced at seeing him broke, like the rest of them. Dennis later recalled their taunts: "My friends kept saying, 'But I thought you were an actor!'"

But the would-be star won points with all of them when his sensational epileptic fit aired on January 5, 1955. Dennis had been crazy with anticipation for weeks before "Boy in the Storm" was broadcast. As the hour approached, he was yelling at his parents to get into the living room to see the show. David Hopper was already there, enthusiastically waiting to see his elder brother reduced to a tiny figure on the tube. As the story unfolded, the family was mesmerized, almost forgetting Dennis was there. David's eyes grew wide with amazement when Dennis, the epileptic, went into his writhing, convulsing fit. It was so convincing that David was scared out of his wits. Their mother remarked, "It's similar to what Granny described when you were sniffing gasoline back on the farm." But they were all impressed by Dennis's performance, which had more impact to them than any of his Shakespearean efforts.

Dennis sat watching with a mixture of embarrassment and deep satisfaction. He enjoyed every moment of seeing himself on the screen but was chagrined that his television debut had been so bizarre. He felt better, however, when his dad told him that his portrayal of the troubled epileptic was sensitive and convincing. Similar sentiments were voiced by his agent, Bob Raison, when he called Dennis the following morning urging him to return to Hollywood right away. Three studios had called already, talking about contracts. He wanted to talk to Dennis immediately about the offers.

By the time Dennis returned, it was even better. Seven major studios were eager to sign him. Sitting in Raison's office, the eighteen-year-old actor felt the first surge of elation that comes with serious recognition. Lighting a cigarette and coolly blowing smoke, he said, "I'm not rushing into anything, let's go over the offers together. I don't want to make a mistake."

Their decision was that Columbia represented the best deal. The agent was ecstatic as they arrived on the Columbia lot. He could see a big future and even bigger bucks in it for both of them if young Hopper fulfilled the promise he had so rapidly demonstrated. The high point of their grand tour around the studio was a brief meeting with Harry Cohn, Columbia's chief. Cohn was a tough and ruthless businessman, a movie mogul who had stars with years of experience quaking when he delivered just a few words of criticism. He was a martinet, managing and manipulating the lives of his stable of stars, controlling every aspect of his movie productions down to the smallest detail. Raison had told his young client how Cohn had crushed all competition, even pushing aside his brother, Jack Cohn, to take total control of Columbia. At sixty-three, he certainly wasn't a man to be trifled with. But that was something this adolescent from Kansas did not understand when he walked cockily into Cohn's outer office.

The massive door to the great man's sanctum was closed. Three nervous secretaries sat at desks busily typing, answering telephones, and mostly turning away the callers who wanted just a word with Cohn. Eventually Cohn buzzed one of his minions to usher Dennis Hopper into his presence. The studio talent scout who accompanied the actor and his agent practically bowed when they completed the long walk from the door to Cohn's desk, a huge semicircular piece of furniture raised on a dais. Behind the moviemaker was an army of Oscars—an arc of shining rainbow light. Cohn looked down on them as they seated themselves in front of him. Dennis felt like a prize bull to be bid on at a Kansas county fair as Cohn said, "I seen your TV show, kid, you got it, you're a natural, like Monty Clift! What else you done?"

Dennis liked the compliment; Clift was one of his heroes. He smiled confidently as he replied, "I've done Shakespeare at the Old Globe. . . ."

There was a slight pause before Cohn sneered, "Shakespeare, oh my God." Then, fixing the talent scout with his cold stare, he added, "Listen, give this kid some cash and put him under contract. Then get him started with a coach to wipe out that Shakespeare crap. I hate Shakespeare." Looking at Dennis, he figured the kid would be thrilled with a cash deal and a contract.

But Dennis was not. His blood ran hot, his mouth went out of control, as he stood up from his chair. Who was this guy taking shots at his best work? He had other offers; he didn't have to take this.

"Go fuck yourself!" The words were out, hanging in the suddenly chilled air. Dennis's agent and the talent scout looked near fainting as Dennis left them behind, walking to the door before the order to throw him out could be given. Over his shoulder he heard Cohn explode, "Don't ever let that bastard set foot in my studio again—or his schlemiel agent. You'll never work at Columbia, not even a crowd scene. . . ."

18

At Warner Brothers, Dennis made a better impression. Fortunately, meeting studio chief Jack Warner was not part of Dennis's itinerary. Instead, he met director Nicholas Ray, who was casting for *Rebel Without a Cause*. He told Hopper he would use him in *Rebel*. It would be a small part, probably no speaking lines, but he would appear in several important scenes. And production executives told him there was a good chance of a bigger part in *Giant*—to be directed by George Stevens. Dennis would be working with James Dean in both pictures.

Warner Brothers signed Hopper to one of their standard seven-year contracts. It meant he would also be doing television for Warner's TV unit as well as movies. Dennis liked the deal. It meant regular work and actually getting paid for doing what he loved best.

He was in the Warner commissary on the second day of the shooting of *Rebel*, killing time. Someone asked him if he wanted to meet James Dean, one of the stars of the movie. Dennis had seen Dean's first picture, *East of Eden*. It was good, but he felt he could equal him in front of the camera.

"Here was this grubby guy, in tennis sneakers, an old turtleneck, and glasses, sitting with a cup of coffee, pouring sugar into it and watching the sugar dissolve," Dennis remembers. "Spoon after spoon he'd pour, always watching it, till the cup was full of sugar. We were introduced and he didn't even turn around, he didn't say hello. That's how he was, man. Honest. If he didn't feel like talking to you he just didn't. Then I got to know him, during *Rebel*, and we found we were so much alike, man, both from farms, this early loneliness, unable to communicate at home, having to create, to justify our lives. He was the most creative person I ever knew, and was twenty years ahead of his time.

"Man, Jimmy and I were into peyote and grass when it

was still like something you couldn't even mention to your closest buddies."

If Dennis had thought he could equal Dean as an actor, the notion died as soon as he saw him working.

"I'd never seen an actor work the way Jimmy did. He was totally transformed when the camera began to roll. He suddenly was the character. There was an integrity, a reality to his acting that couldn't be equaled. Strange things were coming out of him. Because he was working internally and I was working externally. He wasn't repeating. I didn't understand how he was arriving at those conclusions, because he was having real emotional feelings, real emotional reactions."

Dennis would not rest until he had learned some of Dean's secrets. For that reason he approached Dean when they were filming *Rebel*'s "chickie-run" scene. Dean's character, the new kid in town, had been challenged by Buzz, the leader of the gang of teenagers Dennis's character, Goon, belonged to. The two rivals would race cars to the edge of a cliff, then leap out before going over. Whose nerve broke, who jumped out to save himself first, was chicken—the lowest level a teenager in that society could sink to.

Between takes Hopper cornered Dean. "I literally picked him up, threw him into the car, and said, 'What are you doing?' How can I do it? Do I have to go to Strasberg? Do I have to go to New York? Look, man, I gotta know how you act 'cause you're the greatest.'

"Jimmy said, 'No, no, take it easy, man. Just listen to me and I'll help you along. Do things, don't show them. Stop the gestures. In the beginning everything will be very difficult because you're used to acting. But pretty soon it will be natural to you and you'll start going and the emotions will come to you if you leave yourself open to the moment-to-moment reality.'"

Dean fulfilled his promise to help the now-humbled

Hopper. James Dean would be dead the next year, but his mark on Dennis Hopper would be part of the legacy he left to Hollywood.

The pretty young actresses, and there were plenty on the set, didn't escape Dennis's notice, either. He was not one for all work and no play. One pretty little brunette stood out from the rest. And it wasn't just because she was also one of the leads in *Rebel*. Natalie Wood had a special quality, a sweetness mixed with sensuality, that came across in person even better than it did on camera. They began dating while working together on *Rebel*.

Dennis and Natalie were about a year apart in age, just teenagers when they began dating. What started out as a light romance never got much heavier. They did become good friends, although there was still a sexual dimension to the relationship.

Their romance was nothing like the fiery relationship Natalie had spasmodically with Jimmy Dean. He kept her swinging on a manic pendulum. At the high point, she adored him. At the low, he was her tormentor. Dean would mock her appearance, her clothes, her middle-class squareness.

Dennis would just shrug when she discussed his friend's cruelty, and he was happy to step in and comfort her. They were always running into each other through their work. After *Rebel* they appeared in a number of television shows together and were always pleased to be in the same project.

Natalie had many admirers—and lovers—besides Dennis and Jimmy. Nick Adams, another young actor who appeared in *Rebel Without a Cause*, was said to have been her first lover. All of these relationships seemed to flow into and around each other with a minimum of friction. Many of these young men could be found splashing around in a pool at Natalie's home in Sherman Oaks, where she still lived with her family.

Dennis and Natalie had some pretty wild times together. The group of young Hollywood actors they were part of considered themselves the successors to the Barrymores, Errol Flynn, Sinatra, all the high livers of previous generations. And they wanted to be just as outrageous as they had heard their predecessors had been. So they tried to compete with that image, but the reality never seemed to stack up to their imaginations.

In fact, reality could be pretty disastrous at times. One wild night ended with Dennis having to rush Natalie to the hospital emergency room. They, along with Nick Adams and a girlfriend of Natalie's who was dating Adams, had all decided to have an orgy together. None of them had ever actually been to an orgy, so they weren't really quite sure how to begin.

Finally Natalie came up with the idea for getting the show on the road. She said, "To do this right, we have to have a champagne bath." Adams and Dennis, not really having a better idea, agreed to get the champagne. They got a couple of cases and took them back to Dennis's apartment. They had quite a time just uncorking all those bottles to get the bathtub filled.

"Okay, Natalie," they called out, "let's start the orgy!" Natalie, being the bolder of the two girls, went into the bathroom, undressed quickly, and stepped into the bubbling liquid. She tried to look sexy as she slowly lowered herself into the tub. At first it was just cold, but seconds after she sat down she was burning! It felt like red-hot coals had been thrust between her legs. She jumped up, screaming. Her friends didn't know what was wrong or what to do.

She finally made them understand, between cries of pain, saying, "I—am—on—fire." They helped her step out of the tub, over to the sink, and started splashing cold water between her legs. The tears were streaming down Natalie's face and the burning was just getting worse, she said. They had no idea what else to do, or even how serious the problem was. So Dennis got her half-dressed and he and Nick rushed her to the hospital. That was the last time Natalie and Dennis tried to get an orgy going—at least, the last time they tried it together.

Dennis was not idle while Natalie was dating other people. Dennis was a rising young actor—or, as they referred to him at the time, a promising newcomer. His good looks and talent made him attractive to a number of women in the movie business. They included a couple of starlets, Ursula Andress and Joan Collins. But Dennis said of that period in his life, "None of these affairs were too serious. But I don't think there was a starlet around who could have been had in those days that I didn't have." The intensity that had frightened away some of the high-school girls made him all the more attractive to women seeking fame and fortune in Hollywood. They wanted to be with a man reaching for the top.

In addition to the sexual bonanza Dennis was enjoying, he was having a great time hanging out with other young actors and musicians. He and Jimmy would often go to jazz clubs together. His friend loved to try to get into jam sessions, playing the conga drums that he was still taking lessons to master. Dennis's use of drugs increased as he dived enthusiastically into the jazz scene. Jazz and drugs had a lot to say to Dennis. He was intrigued with the improvisational qualities of the music. It was a bit like Dean's Method acting—the same song could be played over and over, but it was always fresh because of the improvisation. The same feeling came through every time, but with a different twist, another variation. It was what he wanted to achieve with his acting. And the drugs made him hear more and feel everything more intensely.

Dennis began to use cocaine, which was to become a

major problem in his later life. But there were also other new drugs to experiment with. He could get the same hallucinatory effects of his childhood gasoline-sniffing experiences from some crazy dried cactus tops, peyote, that were going around. He liked the feeling so much he kept a stock on hand at all times. In those days, a visitor to Dennis's apartment could always find a brew of the drug simmering on the stove. The peyote was a constant fixture in Dennis's life for five years, until he had a bad trip the way he had had with the gasoline sniffing.

An observer of the Hollywood scene, writer Michael St. John, was himself an aspiring young actor in those days and was also a friend of Dean. He said, "I remember Jimmy saying to me, 'I just know if I run into Dennis tonight, he's going to take me on a trip.' This was before that kind of terminology was in common use, and I thought he meant they were going somewhere. He had to explain to me that he meant a trip on drugs."

Alcohol was a big part of the scene as well. Dennis would go to James Dean's house in the San Fernando Valley, a then-rural suburb of Los Angeles. They would get several six-packs of beer, some pot, and spend an afternoon and evening getting high. The sweet smell of pot hung in the air of Dean's little house like a blanket of fog. It was thickened by a tobacco haze from the cigarettes they chain-smoked when they weren't passing round a joint. There, stoned and content, they swapped dreams of a dazzling future, vowed they would always be friends. They were like brothers and had shared many similar past experiences, Jimmy on his uncle's farm in Fairmont, Indiana, Dennis on his grandparents' farm. Both had been lonely and to some degree unhappy during childhood. Dennis had felt the absence of his parents deeply when he was left with his grandparents. It was the same for Dean, who at age eight had been shipped off to live with relatives when his mother died. They had both been gifted art students at school—and still found an outlet for their creativity through drawing and painting. Now, their love of acting had brought them together and they were going to be the best the business had ever seen. They talked, too, about eventually becoming directors—the ultimate expression of film art.

Dennis may have been high as a kite during his discussions with Dean, but he was also picking his pal's brain for everything he could get. He wanted to know, he wanted to feel, he wanted to see just what made James Dean tick dramatically.

Dean had spent some time in New York hanging around the Actors Studio, observing classes. And what he had seen had stayed with him as a powerful influence on his work. It was the Method that he was using every time he got in front of a camera. Dean liked Dennis and was flattered by Hopper's avid attention. Dennis was five years younger and his talent needed developing, but his love of acting and drama matched Dean's. Dean and Dennis would stride about the living room exhaling marijuana fumes and emoting. They would try to terrify each other, screwing up their faces like monsters. They would act out tender love scenes. They were passengers on the sinking Titanic. They were the crew on a plane plunging to the earth far below. They were anything their drug-inflamed imaginations could conjure. But most of all, they were the very best of friends and colleagues.

Dean also got a lot out of the relationship. Emoting with Dennis helped him crystallize some of his theories about acting. The younger man's admiration made him feel more confident; he still had serious doubts about his own talent. To Dennis, it was inconceivable that Dean could be insecure. Jimmy was everything Dennis admired and was a vital influence in demonstrating the power of Method acting to him. In fact, it was James Dean who planted the seeds from which Dennis's career would grow and take its ultimate shape.

Dennis wanted to cut out from Hollywood and go to New York right away, to study at the Actors Studio, to learn the Method. Dean counseled him not to be too eager; there was still much to learn right there in Hollywood. Dean knew from bitter experience that New York was a tough place to make a living while also studying and looking for a break—a role in a stage play, a part in a television drama. Dennis did not want to go back to swiping milk and orange juice from people's porches. Anyway, he was tied contractually to Warner for seven years. And management there didn't give a damn about the Method, they just wanted to keep grinding out movies. Dennis decided Jimmy was right. Besides, soon he would appear in his first substantial movie role, in *Giant*. And he and Dean were looking forward to working together. No need to go rushing off to New York just yet.

Although *Giant* was Dennis's breakthrough movie, few people remember him in it. All attention was focused on such legends as Rock Hudson, Elizabeth Taylor . . . and, of course, Dennis's buddy, James Dean. And it was on *Giant* that Dennis saw another aspect of Dean's personality, a selfish need to hog the limelight and play head games. Dean not only enjoyed throwing stars like Taylor and Hudson into a frenzy of discontent by acting them into the ground, but he also delighted in using their names to grab publicity for himself.

Giant was filmed partly on location in Marfa, Texas, and partly on Warner Brothers' Hollywood sound stages. Dennis played the idealistic, prejudice-fighting son of Rock Hudson and Elizabeth Taylor.

Because of the illustrious company, Dennis came to *Giant* with high anxiety. But the director, George Stevens, was excellent at his job, easily calming Dennis's early jitters. When Dennis saw him approaching, he thought Stevens would immediately start telling him how he wanted the scene played. Instead, Stevens began asking Hopper where he was from and introducing him to the people who were on the set. The next thing Dennis knew, Stevens had him seated on camera and was saying, "Look at the way you're sitting. I like the way you're sitting." Without realizing it, Dennis was in the scene and the cameras were rolling. His anxiety was gone; he felt like he was just continuing the conversation that he'd been having with Stevens.

It was also reassuring for Dennis to know that Dean would watch his work and critique it after the day's filming. Hopper learned a lot about acting this way. Jimmy would tell him about a phantom line that existed on every set. It was an imaginary line separating reality off camera from drama on camera. He would watch what was on the other side of the line for a while, how naturally everyone off camera moved and spoke. Then he would strive to be just as natural on his side of the line, with the camera rolling. Dennis remembered his mentor with admiration: "He was a great teacher. He taught me the trick about the 'imaginary line.' If you go to a movie set you'll notice that the people who are sitting around off camera—the technicians and the visitors and so on—are behaving in one way, and the people who are on camera— that is to say, the 'actors'—are behaving in another. In other words, one is natural and the other is false. Dean knew how to observe what was going on immediately off camera, and how to bring that same tone of reality onto the set itself. And that's what's meant by 'great acting'—because then it isn't acting at all."

Dennis also noted with amusement as Dean played his head games on Elizabeth Taylor and Rock Hudson. Jimmy would mumble his lines, not look at them as he delivered— perfect for his character, but hard for them to follow. He would be watching them slyly out of the corner of his eye as they blew their dialogue. He knew his brooding presence threw them off. The director knew, too, but that was the essence of Dean's performance. There was nothing Stevens could do to correct the problem without ruining the integrity of the character Dean was creating.

Elizabeth and Rock enlisted the help of actress Carroll Baker, who had trained in the Method at the Actors Studio, to give them private lessons in Method acting, but it did not work. Dean still kept stealing their scenes and he and Dennis would laugh about it later.

While at first Elizabeth was complaining about Dean and his thievery before the cameras, soon he was enchanting her personally. She would steal off to meet him, and the rest of the cast and crew did not know where they went and what they did together. They could only assume that Jimmy and Liz were having an affair.

Dennis watched with amazement as Dean calmly pulled this off. Before long Jimmy had both Liz and Rock eating out of the palm of his hand. Every time a newspaper photographer arrived on the set, Jimmy would jump into the picture with Liz. Soon the papers were full of pictures of the pair; it almost looked as though Rock Hudson was playing a supporting role to James Dean.

But Jimmy's game ended when he went too far. One day in front of the press he picked Liz up and turned her upside down so her skirt fell over her head, exposing her panties. Dennis, who in the movie was playing Taylor's son, laughed so hard he almost cried. Liz was red-faced with embarrassment when Dean put her back on her feet. She felt even more humiliated when George Stevens admonished her to behave in a more dignified manner, that she shouldn't let Dean do things like that. The relationship between Dean and Taylor cooled from then on.

The mother-son film relationship between Elizabeth

and Dennis was an odd piece of casting, considering the fact that she was only three years older than Hopper. Rock Hudson played Dennis's father, and together they pulled off a difficult scene which ended with Dennis breaking down sobbing. He glowed when director Stevens complimented him on his work in this scene.

Dennis and Dean's biggest scene together was a fight sequence in which Dean punched Dennis out. They practiced it for hours prior to going before the cameras. Other members of the cast thought they looked like two happy schoolboys feigning rage and anger, perfecting the fight moves. Sometimes they went tumbling over the ground, laughing outrageously.

The film was finished in September 1955, with the final scenes shot in Los Angeles. Jimmy was especially happy because he was back behind the wheel of his Porsche, which he had been banned from driving. Prescient studio executives were fearful that their star might have an accident during production because of his love of speed. Like kids let out from school, Hopper and Dean jumped into the speedster and rode, laughing and shouting, to the Villa Capri for a dinner celebrating the last day of shooting on *Giant*. Jimmy was bubbling with enthusiasm for the big race in Salinas, where he hoped to win with a Porsche Spyder that was being fine-tuned for the event. Dennis was bored by Dean's talk of cars and was relieved when conversation turned to the movie they had just made.

Dennis later recalled: "That night we were downtown in the old restaurant Sinatra used to go to, Villa Capri. And Dean said, 'I saw what you did today in your scene with Hudson. I wish Edmund Kean could have seen you. And John Barrymore. Because today you were great.' And I started to tear up. And tears started coming down my face. He said, 'It's very sweet. You're showing appreciation for what I'm saying, but when you really become a fucking actor you'll have to leave the room to cry. Then you'll be there. . . .'"

CHAPTER FOUR

James Dean's death on September 30, 1955, shattered Hopper. He reacted violently. A well-meaning friend heard the news in a radio report and rushed over to Dennis's home to inform him personally. Hopper had been sleeping off a hangover when he answered the urgently ringing doorbell to hear the man babbling something about Dean being dead. Dennis went mad, slamming the bearer of bad tidings against the wall, then hitting him in the mouth as though to silence the shocking words.

Dennis later recalled: "It was horror; it was unbelievable. I didn't mean to do it. I was screaming, 'Don't you ever put me on like that again, man!'" But it was no joke; Dean was gone. Hopper turned on the radio and the station was spilling out the story. Jimmy's speeding Porsche Spyder had crashed broadside into a Ford that had turned across the path of the actor's car. They had found him trapped in the car, his head hanging over at a horrible right angle, his neck broken.

A nurse who had been one of the first people to stop at the crash site felt Dean's wrist and there was a slight pulse, but the eyes were unfocused. When the ambulance men arrived, they had trouble getting him out of the wreck. As they lifted the torn body Jimmy seemed to stir suddenly, almost as if he was going to say something. There was a small convulsive stiffening, and a rasping sound from his lips. It was the air leaving Jimmy's lungs. His head fell over completely as he died. The Spyder had come to rest, after a number of cartwheels, right-side-up fifteen feet off the highway. The hood had sprung open and the trunk gaped wide, exposing the hot engine in the rear. The left side was mashed like a swatted insect; the right was almost undamaged. Jimmy's passenger, a mechanic, had been thrown out of the car and was alive, though badly injured. They had been on the way to the Salinas races Jimmy had talked about so enthusiastically during his last dinner with Dennis. Witnesses said that before the impact, Dean had been driving at high speed; some estimated the car had been moving as fast as 130 miles an hour. Before hitting the Ford, another automobile had been forced off the road to avoid the Spyder as it flashed along.

Dennis wondered if his friend had been high at the time of the accident: He was a fast driver but not that reckless. At nineteen, death was incomprehensible to Hopper; he and Dean thought themselves immortal. Dennis had believed up to then that truly talented people were allowed to live until they fulfilled their promise. Gone in an instant were their dreams of acting and directing together. So much had hinged on what he and Jimmy had planned together. It was not fair. Dennis felt betrayed, cheated by death. He collapsed in a flood of tears; now he saw how treacherous life could be.

"His death blew my mind. I couldn't get it together, man, for a long time afterward. Because I really believed in predestination, that something protected gifted people until they could realize their potential. Jimmy was going to direct, and he would have been great. It was the worst personal tragedy in my life, it affected me for years after. The guy was always with me. Every time I walked onto a sound stage, he was there watching every move I made, listening to every word I uttered. I was still trying to live up to what I'd learned from him. Guess I always will," Hopper told an interviewer years later. The briefness of the relationship did not negate its profoundly lasting effect on Dennis.

Dennis and Natalie Wood turned to each other for whatever comfort they could find. He had to be around people who had known Dean and understood how great he was. At first he couldn't stand the questions of the morbidly curious who had never known Dean and were descending like vultures to pick his bones now that he was dead. With Natalie there were no stupid questions. She had known and loved Dean also, and she knew how important, almost sacred, the friendship was between the two young men. She understood how Dennis felt. Together they could comfort one another, crying and occasionally laughing when they remembered some of the good times. At moments they were just completely quiet, holding one another. Best of all, they did not have to explain anything.

A few days after Dean's death, *Rebel Without a Cause* opened in theaters all over the country. The James Dean craze was just beginning, even though his life was over. Usually the opening of a young actor's first film is a joyful occasion, but for Dennis, Dean's death cast a shadow that dimmed the glittering occasion.

The funeral took place far from Hollywood, in Indiana, near the Dean family home. Dennis felt there was an unreal quality to his friend's death—it was more like a disappearance than a death. There they had been, having dinner together at the Villa Capri. Dean had driven away, forever. What was left of him, his earthly remains, had been put in a casket and flown back to Indiana, and Dennis would never see him again. Worse, Dean's unique talent was gone. While waiting for the reality of death to sink in, Dennis went through the motions of everyday life in a daze.

For a while he was bothered by fans who would write him letters, not about his work, but because they knew he had been close to Dean and had questions they wanted Dennis to answer. After a while it ceased to bother him. Even the already famous were fascinated with the legend of Jimmy Dean. Elvis Presley came to Hollywood the year after Dean's death, and he sought out Dennis because of his connection with Jimmy. Dennis later recalled their meeting:

"When Elvis Presley first came to Hollywood to make a movie, he came to see me. He was twenty-one and a millionaire. He had seen James Dean in *Rebel Without a Cause* . . . and he wanted to know more about Jimmy. We were talking about movies, and he said he didn't see how he could hit the actress who was going to play opposite him. I said, 'Just pretend you're slapping at a bothersome fly.' But he said, 'No, I can't hit a woman!' and I suddenly realized that it wasn't a question of motivation. Elvis actually believed that he had to hit the girl in this scene!

"He had to fight another actor, too, he said, but he was in pretty good shape and thought he could take care of him. I explained that you never actually hit anyone in a movie, that it was all faked but the film was cut in such a way as to give the impression that it actually happened. Elvis was angry. He thought I was kidding him; he couldn't accept the fact that he had been deceived all these years by movies."

Dennis continued as he felt Dean would have wanted. In the eyes of the industry, he took on the mantle of the rebel, but he definitely had a cause. His rebellion was against the movie business establishment and the way they made films. He rebelled against old-style directors, who didn't know the first thing about Method acting. They demanded that actors do as they were told, stop trying to give their own interpretation of each role.

But Dennis wasn't all rebel. Some of the glamour of the business held an attraction for him, and he was still such a newcomer that he could get involved in the excitement of going to movie premieres, especially for the first movie in which he had a large speaking part. When *Giant* premiered, he took Natalie Wood as his officially sanctioned studio date. The executives didn't care that he and Natalie had a real relationship going—the public-relations people had decided being seen together was good for both their careers.

Going into the theater, Dennis displayed some discomfort when Natalie stopped to pose for the press and insisted on kissing him in front of the photographers; she looked lovingly up at him while he kept one eye on the cameras. Even though she was younger than Dennis, Natalie was already an old pro in studio publicity—she'd been a child star for years. There was a phoniness to it that was beginning to get on Hopper's nerves. Luckily the hungry reporters soon went after the real stars of the movie, Elizabeth Taylor and Rock Hudson, and took the glaring lights off the youngsters.

They made a good-looking couple, in spite of Dennis's awkwardness. And so did David Hopper and Lana Wood, the stars' younger brother and sister. The kids went along to the premiere on a double date with Dennis and Natalie. This was the type of publicity stunt the studios loved to pull off, but the younger Hopper and Wood kids were oblivious to being used and Dennis and Natalie didn't mind giving their younger siblings a night to remember.

But Dennis found he did not like being told who he should take to movie premieres. His rebellious nature took over and he infuriated studio chiefs when he refused to take Natalie to the New York opening of *Giant*. On that occasion he thought they were trying to exploit a personal relationship for publicity purposes. They wanted to get newspaper attention, building up the suggestion that he and Natalie were having a hot affair, when in fact their romance had ended and they were now just good friends. Natalie was being a trouper and was ready to go along with what her bosses wanted. But the phoniness of the plan nauseated Dennis, who just didn't want to be used this way, no matter how it annoyed Natalie or the men in charge. Instead, he took Joanne Woodward, a then-unknown stage performer.

Joanne agreed to go to the premiere with Dennis because it was the first big motion picture opening she had attended. Dennis later told an interviewer about that night: "I went to the premiere of *Giant*, and the studio wanted me to take Natalie, and I wanted to take Joanne Woodward, and nobody had ever heard of Joanne Woodward, and I insisted. So when I arrived at the premiere of *Giant*, they wouldn't interview me because I was with Joanne Woodward, and they said, 'Who are you, his secretary?'"

After the movie, Joanne and Dennis went to a party at the Copacabana nightclub. They sat at Jack Warner's table, where all the attention was focused on Elizabeth Taylor. Dennis told Joanne not to worry about being ignored, the people doing the ignoring were a bunch of phonies. He was outraged, too, because Mike Todd kept insisting that Dennis go and find Elizabeth, who was flitting around the room and missing most of the evening. Irritated, Joanne asked Dennis to take her home. When he tried to follow her through the door of her apartment, she held her arm up to bar him. When he didn't budge, Hopper recalls, "Finally she pushed me down a flight of stairs. I never figured that out, until later she told me that Paul [Newman] was waiting for her in her apartment."

His rebellious attitude escalated and he began to direct his temperamental flare-ups at anyone who represented the straight establishment to him. Hopper's outspoken rudeness annoyed aging songwriter Cole Porter at a lavish party. "I got so fed up with everyone agreeing with Mr. Porter that I blew up and told them off, told them what I thought of them. Mr. Porter promptly asked me to leave, but later wrote me a very nice letter," Dennis recalls. "He said I was right about the sycophants, but that he was too old and had gone too far to put up with such behavior from a young punk who hadn't proven himself yet."

But worse was yet to come. Warner Brothers Studio loaned Dennis to 20th Century-Fox to play the role of one of the sons of a villain. Hopper soon turned the set of *From Hell to Texas* into a battleground. There he butted heads with one of the toughest directors in the business: Henry Hathaway, a veteran from the old school. Hathaway had worked up to directing the hard way, from the bottom rungs of the studio ladder. He had started as a studio carpenter and had made the long climb to director. He thought he knew about acting because he'd done a few juvenile roles as a young man. Hathaway was a seasoned warrior, in front of and behind the camera, by the time he clashed with young Dennis.

"I walked off the picture three times," Dennis recalls. "I wouldn't take direction. He wanted me to imitate Marlon Brando; he'd say, 'Say it like this: aaaayeeeeuh, hey man, aahduuh,' and I'd say, 'I don't want to do that, I'm trying to get away from that, and please don't give me line readings. I'm a Method actor. I work with my ears, my sight, my head, and my sense of smell.'" Each time Hopper walked off, Hathaway would take him to dinner and promise to let Dennis have his way if he would return to the set the next morning. But the guileful veteran did not keep his word.

"The next day he would come on the set and say, 'Forget what I said last night; it's fucking dinner talk.' On the set he was a monster, screaming and yelling," Hopper claims.

Incredibly, they arrived at the last day of shooting.

"I had a ten-line scene with the actor who played my father, and Hathaway came on the set and said, 'You know what those things are over there?' And I said, 'Yeah, those are film cans.' He said, 'Yeah, those are film cans. There's enough film in there to shoot for four months. And you're going to do the scene my way. You're gonna pick up the coffee cup and put it down. You're gonna read the lines this way. And you can do it that way or you can just make a career out of this one scene in this one movie. Because I own forty percent of this studio. We're here now to stay. We'll send out for lunch, send out for dinner, we're here. Sleeping bags will be brought in. This is it.'"

This was seven in the morning. By midmorning, a production head at Warner's called over to Fox to speak to Dennis. He wanted to know what the hang-up was. Dennis told him. He said, "Cut the crap, Dennis. Just do what Hathaway says and get back over here."

Lunch was brought in. They ate and went back to work. The battle of wills continued. Neither Dennis nor Hathaway had budged an inch. At two o'clock Jack Warner called. His message was the same as his production head's had been: "Do what fucking Hathaway says and get back over here!" The more they pushed, the more Dennis dug in his heels.

Hathaway would scream at Dennis, but Dennis would turn and pretend to be ignoring him, and desperately try to come up with another way to play the scene.

"I did what seemed like eighty-seven different versions of the scene. I played it as comedy—I played it as pathos—I had the crew in tears! Everybody wanted to go home."

They took another break and had dinner brought in. The crew was exhausted and disgusted with this clash of egos. But it was fascinating at the same time. Even people who weren't strictly needed on the set were hanging around, curious to see how this contest would turn out.

Finally, after fifteen hours and eighty-six takes of the

scene, Dennis was the one to cave in. He just couldn't think of another way to do the scene; he was emotionally wrung out. He broke down in tears and said to Hathaway, "Just tell me, one more time, tell me what you want me to do." Hathaway smiled with triumph as he gave him the direction. Dennis did the scene as required.

At the end of the eighty-seventh take, Hathaway yelled, "Cut! That's a wrap." Dennis began to walk off the set. Hathaway yelled after him, "Hey, kid! I want to make you a promise." Dennis turned to look at him and Hathaway continued, "I can promise you one thing. You will never work in this town again! I guarantee it!"

After that Dennis got very little work. Major studios wouldn't offer him parts and he scorned television. He let his hair grow down to his shoulders, chummed around with Beat poet Allen Ginsberg and artist Andy Warhol, announced a Marlon Brando for President campaign, wept in public about "what's happening to my life," and then, to the horror of Hollywood's establishment, eventually married into its inmost circle.

As much as they appreciated Dennis's talent, some Warner Brothers executives were questioning whether it was worth the agony it took to get it on screen. It was common knowledge in Hollywood that the studio did not want to give him another motion picture. They were pushing him toward the more controlled environment of television. They hoped he would mellow and respond to the stringent production demands of that medium.

For his part, Dennis did not really care what Hollywood was planning for his future. He wasn't impressed with what they had done with his talent since *Giant*. Besides the Hathaway fiasco, there had been minor parts in forgettable films, including a performance that was almost lost in a huge pageant, *The Story of Mankind*, which proposed to tell the entire history of humanity. Dennis had been cast as Napoleon Bonaparte, and the part required more posing than acting.

If this was their idea of what to do with a talented young actor, he had had enough. His priority was to get out of his contract, go to New York, and study with Lee Strasberg at the Actors Studio. Hopper placed honing his craft above quick riches and trashy movie fame. He reasoned that he'd really be somebody to be reckoned with once he had solid stage experience. He was tired of being pushed around by the old-guard studio establishment.

So when they offered him the chance to play Billy the Kid in a twice-monthly TV series, he declined. Faced with this impasse, Warner released him from his contract. Other young actors struggling for a break said Dennis Hopper was crazy.

CHAPTER FIVE

New York was everything Dennis had thought it was on his previous visits, only better now that he was living there. He completely dedicated himself to enhancing his skills. For a solid two years he studied the Method with Lee Strasberg at the Actors Studio. To support himself he appeared in numerous television roles, "strictly for the bread, man." He lovingly retraced what he knew of Jimmy Dean's steps when he was in New York; he again felt close to his friend that way.

Dennis was developing himself as an artist; he saw himself as a twentieth-century Renaissance man. New York City was the capital of the modern art world, and he took advantage of all the museums and galleries.

"I became a gallery bum the way some guys are surfing bums or tennis bums," Dennis said. "I learned everything I know at the Museum of Modern Art. I used to go every day, go through the permanent collection until I knew every painting."

While he was developing his artistic eye, he was also developing friendships with many of the artists.

During the day he was at the galleries or in the studios of Andy Warhol, Jasper Johns, Roy Lichtenstein, Edward Kienholz. At night he was hanging out in the jazz clubs. He listened to and got to know the great jazz players like Thelonius Monk and Miles Davis. He loved the music and the whole scene surrounding it: women, drugs, liquor, and the after-hours clubs. Decadence and sleaze appealed to him. He sought out the hard drinkers, the druggies who would stay up all night with him. Dennis could drink beer, martinis, or brandy till dawn and still be standing. Finally he had found a city that didn't close down just as he was loosening up. And he had found a group of people, or enough different groups of people, to hang with so that he didn't ever have to be alone.

Dennis was also busy with another new interest: photography. Everywhere he went, he took a camera with him. His friends began calling him "the Tourist." Jimmy Dean had recommended photography to Dennis as a way to develop his artistic vision. Now he consciously set out to use photography as a training ground for his directorial eye.

He experimented with different types of film, and with color as well as black and white, until he made a choice to use only one type of film, Tri-X black and white. Tri-X was a fast film that allowed him to shoot in a variety of situations using only available light. At first he used a light meter to get readings, soon abandoned it when he found it slowed him down and that when he was taking pictures of people, they tended to get distracted with his process as a photographer rather than relating to him and the camera directly.

Dennis also made the decision not to crop his pictures after developing them. Cropping was not a luxury a movie director would have. A director had to get a shot framed properly to begin with or it was no good. There was no going in afterward to fix it. He started out doing still life studies of everyday objects, then expanded into taking pictures of his artist friends: painters, actors, musicians, poets. His photos eventually caught the interest of magazines like *Vogue* and *Harper's Bazaar*, where his work was first published.

His friend, writer Terry Southern, later remembered the scene in New York among the artists and intellectuals where he first saw Dennis:

"I remember several years back my first meeting with Hopper—at the outlandish East Fifth Street pad of Allen Ginsberg and Peter Orlovsky—during what must have been one of the first 'happenings' ever to occur in New York City. Orlovsky was playing on some sort of strange Eastern timpani, and chanting sotto voce, 'Blood in the milk, blood in the milk, blood in the milk . . .' while Allen, dipping a rolled copy of *The New York Times Book Review* into a large can of honey, inscribed hauntingly cryptic word-images across the far wall. In one corner a movie projector was rattling away, showing Luis Buñuel's *L'Age d'Or* in reverse, but was focused through an open door, so that nothing could be seen except when someone happened to pass through the stream of shuttering light. In the center of the room an electric fan was lying on its back, blades up, whirling violently—and crouched beside it was a marvelous stark-naked Negro girl of about twenty, holding a huge paper sack from which she took what was apparently a mixture of rose petals and dog hair and dropped them into the fan, so that the room was like a kind of silent snowstorm, all slow motion, the people moving about as in the softest dream. It was pretty weird, now that I think about it. And Hopper—who even then was probably one of the most talented actors alive—became quite excited by the spectacle and eager to take part, gliding around in a Marcel Marceau manner, grimacing oddly and, at the same time, attempting to take photographs with a 135-millimeter Nikon."

In 1959, Hollywood lured Dennis back for a year. He

signed a contract with MGM studios, a five-year deal. He would only be paid when he actually made a picture, according to the terms of the deal. He went back west to appear as a gang leader in the movie *Key Witness*. Hollywood still didn't know quite how to deal with him. While back in the movie capital, he did little to dispel the reputation of being difficult that hung over him like a bad smell after *From Hell to Texas*.

Now, fully immersed in the Method, he was even less willing to take orders from directors accustomed to treating actors like retarded kids; he was always discussing his desire to direct. Thirty years ago, it was practically unheard of for an actor to direct, unlike in the 1980s when it has become commonplace. Actors who became successful directors, like Elia Kazan, were the exceptions in the 1950s.

While still studying at the Actors Studio, Hopper was now occasionally getting work in theater. He was rehearsing for the play *Mandingo* when he met Brooke Hayward, a shy, sensitive, well-bred young woman who was the divorced mother of two children she was raising as a single parent. A year younger than Dennis, she had long dark hair, a lovely pale complexion, and lips that easily formed a sensuous pout when she was deep in thought.

Brooke, who had lived in the shadow of her late mother, Margaret Sullavan, a great Broadway and movie actress, wanted to follow in her footsteps, but she doubted her own ability. Her father was Leland Hayward, who was first a great Hollywood agent, then a major theatrical producer. Brooke's family and friends were Hollywood royalty. Brooke succeeded on her own in a modeling career, reaching the prestigious status of *Vogue* magazine cover girl at age twenty-two. Now she was back to pursuing the acting career she had studied for.

Dennis had a leading role in the play *Mandingo*, while Brooke had the part of his wife. Her beauty and talent touched him deeply, he was impressed by her background.

She had grown up as a part of that Hollywood glamour that, in turns, attracted him, then caused him to rebel. He began to court Brooke while the play was still in rehearsals. By the time *Mandingo* opened, they were romantically involved off-stage as well as on. The play flopped, closing a mere two days after it opened, but their love affair flourished.

Brooke was a shrewd judge of the theatrical scene, having lived with it all her life. She had strong convictions and a sure knowledge of what was good and bad about the work of other actors, although unsure of her own performances. Dennis valued her opinions and was deeply flattered when she told him how much she admired his style and originality.

Brooke had a tragic air about her that also attracted Dennis. In 1960 her mother had died of an overdose of barbiturates while working out of town on a play bound for Broadway. So the couple had another bond; they had both recently lost people they loved and admired.

Dennis had been involved with many different women, had enjoyed a lot of sex, but he had not been seriously in love. Thoughts of marriage had never stirred in him until he met Brooke. He felt slightly awed by her. She demanded he take her seriously or leave her alone. She warned wayward Dennis she wanted a respectable family life. That if they married, he would have to clean up his life-style. He had to consider the influence he would have on her sons. He agreed. Yet, while she worried about Dennis's untamed behavior, she was attracted to the wildness she saw in him. She adored his tilting at the establishment, his crazy irreverent sense of humor, his love of art, his total dedication to his craft. Her sons, Willie, three, and Jeffrey, four, romped and played with Hopper, and the notion of having a ready-made family appealed to him. He began to love the little boys. He wanted to give them a good life, to encourage their growth, their ambitions. He would be a loving parent to these trusting kids and they would return that love. That was his vision for the future with them and Brooke.

On August 9, 1961, Dennis and Brooke were married. The reception was held in the New York apartment of Brooke's friend since childhood, Jane Fonda. On the day of the wedding, Brooke's father called at 6 A.M. to remind her there was still time to call it off. Neither he nor Brooke's stepmother approved of Hopper or the way he lived, dressed, talked. Everything about him was horrific to them. But through Brooke, Dennis got to know the Fonda family well and his friendship with Peter Fonda would later lead to his biggest movie success and a turning point in his career.

Soon after their marriage the Hoppers decided to return to Hollywood, where Dennis hoped to resuscitate his movie career. But in the six years that followed, Dennis was sidetracked from this ambition by his other artistic interests and by a slide into drugs and the "Love Generation." Although Brooke had family friends and connections in the Hollywood establishment who could have helped Hopper, they were of little use because he turned them off with his rebellious posturing. As a result, the only roles that came were in schlock movies, like *Queen of Blood*. In this gem of a classically bad science fiction horror movie, Dennis played one of three astronauts who rescue an alien from a space crash. The alien is a sickly greenish woman who feeds on blood and lays eggs. Before the end of the movie, she bleeds Dennis dry. The film wasn't Hopper's idea of art, but it helped finance his family's move west.

The Hoppers moved into a canyon home in ritzy Bel Air furnished mostly with valuable pieces that had belonged to Brooke's mother, and where Dennis had a studio for his painting and photography. There he worked on hundreds of canvases, some of which had been started during his stay in New York. He continued to enhance his reputation as a painter. Several of his actor friends who were enjoying more success than he, such as Joanne Woodward, owned some of his paintings.

By now it was difficult for many people to tell where Hopper's main creative thrust was headed.

"Photographers always thought of me as an actor, painters thought of me as a photographer, and actors . . . well, Paul Newman would say to me, 'You should really concentrate on your painting,'" he observed self-deprecatingly.

The truth was that Hopper had won respect in all three fields and was seeking to put his package of talents together as a film director. But it would be years before that ambition became reality.

Brooke's frustration mounted as she saw the man she had married squander his efforts on other artistic endeavors while neglecting what she believed to be his true talent: theatrical filmmaking. She also found his mercurial personality and use of drugs desperately difficult to live with. Soon after they arrived in California she had a frightening demonstration of his irresponsibility when a raging fire threatened their home.

Just months after they moved to Bel Air, Brooke became scared when she smelled the first whiff of smoke from a fire in the next canyon. She understood the menace of fires in the dry California hills, while apparently Dennis did not.

A dry wind was carrying ashes through the air. She was frightened for her family but was trying to stay calm. She would later tell how their neighbor across the street was watching through binoculars as the fire made its way up their canyon. She saw him hurriedly packing a car with his most valued possessions. She thought she and Dennis should begin doing the same. But he was sleeping when she ran into the house to awaken him. Bleary-eyed, he failed to appreciate or refused to accept the gravity of the situation. She told her husband that their neighbor was loading his car to get out. Later she said Dennis replied, "Ask him to wake us when he gets ready to leave. Tell him on no account to leave without waking us." With that the actor went back to sleep, ignoring his frightened wife. But soon he was awakened again by Brooke's screams and they finally evacuated. By then, there was no time to save anything. Brooke later recalled, "We lost everything. A huge, lovely house, paintings, all my clothes, furniture . . . well, just everything."

Dennis's paintings were gone along with hundreds of poems he had written, mostly during his time in New York. Luckily for his photographic work, all the boxes of negatives were out of the house in preparation for his first gallery showing.

The Hopper family eventually resettled in a more modest Spanish-style home in West Hollywood, in the foothills north of Sunset Boulevard. At the new home Dennis's mark was on everything. He filled the house to suit his eclectic taste, a mixture of modern art and pop-culture icons. There were paintings and sculpture by modern and pop artists like Frank Stella, Roy Lichtenstein, Ed Kienholz, and Andy Warhol. These were displayed alongside antique carousel horses. And old labels from cigar boxes and fruit cans decorated cabinet doors. There was even a fire hydrant stashed in the living room.

The entrance hall featured a mirrored-ball refracting light that played over the small Hammond organ in that hall. There, Dennis once took pictures of singing duo Ike and Tina Turner, Ike seated at the organ, Tina bent over a tub and an old washboard, pretending to scrub a shirt. (When looking at that picture years later, Dennis joked, "Doesn't he look as if he's saying, 'I sure wish I hadn't been beatin' on her,'" referring to Tina Turner's revelations that she had left Ike after enduring years of physical abuse from him.)

Many of the windows of the house were Art Nouveau—style stained glass, one of the original features that attracted Dennis. Furnished with a mixture of European and

Mexican pieces, the home reflected the couple's varied tastes. The outstanding feature of the living room was a fourteen-foot-long papier-mâché clown from Mexico, suspended overhead from the ceiling. A friend said their bedroom ended up looking a bit like whorehouse revival; the bed was a huge Italian brass four-poster production with an ornate headboard. It was hung with sailcloth curtains. On top of the bed was a red and gold cut-velvet spread. Next to the bed was a throne-style chair that had been spirited away from a studio prop department. It was an ideal surrounding for Dennis's hallucinatory trips.

Although being married to Brooke Hayward provided the perfect entrée to the Hollywood power brokers, Dennis blew the opportunity of availing himself of those who could help his film career. Instead, he delighted in shocking and insulting them. There were whispers of "poor Brooke" whenever the name of Hopper came up in conversation. Mrs. Hopper fled from many an important party red-faced and furious after one of her husband's rampages. He had not changed from the time when he hurled insults at Cole Porter's ultrasophisticated party guests. Everyone who knew him had tired of his babbling about the way he and James Dean would have run the movie industry, about how old-guard directors and producers would not have been able to get a job in the studio mail room.

He had complaints against the film establishment. In part referring to the industry's obsession with business rather than art and their willingness to concentrate on profits from studio tours instead of making movies, Dennis wrote: "And who needs Disneyland-with-glass-sound-stages-so-people-can-watch Studios? Props? Heavy equipment? Thirty people on a crew? Three dollars and seventy-five cents an hour for an old man who opens a door and sweeps cigarette butts off the floor and makes coffee (as a matter of fact great coffee), and when he dies (and he won't quit before), his son will take over and do the chore of opening and closing the door."

He would sneeringly tell them: "Jimmy was the most talented and original actor I ever saw work, no matter what you guys think. He was a guerrilla artist who attacked all the restrictions on his sensibility that you imposed. Once he pulled a switchblade and threatened to murder his director. I follow his style in art and life."

Brooke recalled those embarrassing days: "We'd go to these parties where you'd have the crème de la crème of Hollywood, and he'd tell them that when he ran things heads were going to roll, they'd be in chains. Some day he'd make a movie and the old dinosaurs would be slain."

Mrs. Hopper would often spend the day after a party calling to make apologies to their hosts of the night before and sometimes to other guests as well if Dennis had singled them out for individual attention. Many of these people had been friends of her mother and father and had known Brooke all her life. They sympathized with Brooke for being married to "that madman."

In 1962 Dennis and Brooke had a daughter, Marin, and it was Brooke's fervent hope that fatherhood would calm Hopper down. While Dennis was delighted with the little girl and fascinated by her, the other influences in his life remained dominant. There was too much happening out in the streets; Hopper felt that he had to be out there with the people.

"The Sixties was just one big drug party. We experimented for everybody. Free love, be-ins, love-ins, drop in, drop out, take some acid. I dropped in and dropped out," he recalled.

"I heard more about the orgies in the Sixties in Hollywood than I actually participated in. I did have a lot of scenes with two women and myself . . . on the road of excess.

There was a lot of free love. Everyone was going through a period of time where you didn't have to be tied down. I mean, love-ins were people making love. I never participated in the exhibitionistic part of it, the ceremonies. But it was happening. And during the time of LSD it was like you didn't know if you were inside, outside, or alone. And it didn't really matter."

Hopper's use of drugs and alcohol was staggering; his friends were amazed that he lived through it. There was always beer or hard liquor. But he admitted experimenting with hallucinogenics, barbiturates, and speed. He used something to bring him up, followed by something to bring him down so he could cope, followed by something to bring him back up when he began to crash.

Dennis would later say, "I felt that if the great artists had done it, that it must lead into something. It does help you with your senses, and makes your senses like raw nerves. I was working with my nerves."

By 1965, Hopper's focus was on social causes. He had long ago seen how influential motion pictures could be in the lives of average people. He had spoken out in the press as early as 1959 about the preponderance of violence in movies. His motivation for speaking out was partly selfish: He didn't want to be typecast in violent character roles, but he saw his career heading that way. Later he would tell a reporter, "For fifteen years in Hollywood the only role I was able to play was that of a neurotic killer. Kill my mother, kill my father, kill them in bed while they were asleep. Kill strangers, kill somebody, all the time, in one TV show after another. All the producers were concerned with was: Does this picture have enough violence?"

So Hopper took a stand on the side of nonviolence. He was impressed by what the Rev. Martin Luther King, Jr., was doing in the South for civil rights. He believed in the cause, and he also admired the commitment to achieve equality through nonviolent means.

Hopper packed his cameras and headed south to witness firsthand what was happening with the civil rights movement. He participated in the march from Selma to Montgomery, Alabama. It was a grueling five-day trek, much of it through rain and mud. It was a great adventure for Dennis. A good story and some great photographs at the cost of a few days of discomfort. The pictures he did of Dr. King and the other marchers were striking. And redneck southerners spit on him, calling the actor a long-haired, nigger-loving Communist. In the end he knew he was privileged. He didn't have to be black and stay in the South. He felt the enormous contrast when he returned to fantasy land, to make a movie.

At this point Dennis needed to make a movie; he hadn't had a decent part for eight years. It was ironic that his old adversary, director Henry Hathaway, was the vehicle for his temporary comeback. Hathaway rescinded his 1957 promise that Hopper would never work again in a studio with him. He knew of the actor's marriage and thought matrimony would have mellowed the stubborn young man. Dennis reported, "He told me that he had heard that I had married Margaret Sullavan's daughter and that she was a nice Irishwoman." Hathaway gave him a part in *The Sons of Katie Elder*, a Western starring John Wayne, to be filmed in Mexico.

Before shooting started, the director surprised Hopper by saying, "You probably never thought you'd see me on the other side of a camera directing you again, and maybe I'm crazy, but I admire your spunk, kid, and I guess you're not all bad. . . ." Then he added a caution: "And you're not going to make any trouble like you did before, right? This is a

Big Duke picture, and the Duke don't understand that Method shit. Got it?"

Dennis smiled and went to work. He, "Duke" Wayne, and Dean Martin, another co-star, hit it off, sinking a lot of booze. There were many mornings when Hathaway greeted the bleary-eyed trio warily. But he didn't mind the red eyes as long as Dennis performed as promised, without trouble and sans the Method.

The remainder of the 1960s produced minor parts in major movies for Hopper. Although he was excellent in those roles, it was not the stuff he and Jimmy Dean had dreamed about. For example, he was one of the supporting players in Paul Newman's *Cool Hand Luke*. But he wasn't getting the big breaks, the big parts that would really let him strut his stuff. And his dream of directing seemed to be receding further into the distance.

Not only would Hollywood spurn any moves toward directing, but the establishment there was scared to death of Dennis Hopper. Who wanted to risk millions by putting this wild man in big-budget movies and starring roles? His image was a disaster; Dennis knew that and did nothing to improve it. Instead, he retreated still further into the fringe world he had created around himself, a place populated by hippies and artists.

After doing *The Sons of Katie Elder*, Hopper and another writer co-wrote a script, *The Last Movie*, for which he sought producers. The idea for the project came out of his location work in Mexico with Hathaway. After the completion of location work for *The Sons of Katie Elder*, a fully constructed western town was left by the film company for the natives of an agricultural village on the outskirts of Durango, Mexico. Dennis registered an original story that told what happened to a small Mexican village when Hollywood arrived in its midst. The central character was a wrangler who stayed behind when the rest of the cast and crew return to Hollywood. Through the film Dennis would try to show the effects of moviemaking on a relatively primitive people. Hopper was despondent when he couldn't find support—however, six years later, he spent two years making this film.

Hopper now turned to movies that featured drugs and motorcycles, low-budget features made away from the mainstream studio system. The movies weren't great art but they were financially successful, doing solid business with the kids who couldn't relate to products from the big studios, which were still making films about Tammy and Gidget. Dennis starred in *The Glory Stompers*, a box office success with a biker theme. Another film was *The Trip*, written by fellow actor Jack Nicholson. In it Hopper played a drug dealer who sold LSD to Peter Fonda. Dennis and Peter went into the desert and shot the acid trip sequences by themselves.

Brooke was depressed over the direction Dennis's career was now taking. It was a far cry from the goals they had shared when they met in New York and she told him how much she respected his artistry. But she drew some comfort from the fact that at least he was working. Their marriage was in bad trouble, although Hopper didn't take her threats of divorce seriously. They got along better when he was filming because he was away so much. Neither she nor the children were confronted with his daily drug abuse.

The civil rights marches and the abuse from bigots scared Hopper and turned him from a believer in nonviolence to a collector of guns and a karate student.

The ugliness of redneck reactions to anyone different, hate for anything that challenged their life-style, made him doubt that any fair outcome would be achieved through peaceful means. He began to have delusions of himself as a revolutionary, believing the CIA or the FBI were after him. Friends said he would sometimes stalk his neighborhood late at night, gun in hand, in search of government agents he was convinced were spying on him. He even began to turn his persecution delusions on Brooke, screaming that she was part of the conspiracy, that he couldn't trust her. Brooke became increasingly frightened. He had a black belt in karate and was becoming violent with her. Another time, under the influence of drugs, he kicked out the windshield of a neighbor's car. More than for herself, she became frightened of the effect his violent behavior would have on the children.

Ironically, it was *Easy Rider* that finally pushed their marriage into the divorce court. Although it was to become Dennis's biggest success, Brooke hated the script, which was written by Hopper, Peter Fonda, and Terry Southern. She saw it as another in his long run of "biker-druggie movies."

Brooke sued for divorce in March 1967, claiming her husband had a violent temper, used drugs, and struck her on several occasions. She also charged him with "extreme cruelty." On hearing about the divorce, her father called to congratulate her on the "first smart move you've made in six years." The judge issued a restraining order to prevent Hopper from "harassing, annoying, or molesting her." She asked for support and custody of their child, Marin, who was then nearly five.

The divorce papers showed that after thirteen years as an actor, Hopper was worth a mere $10,000 in cash. In the final settlement, Brooke got child support, the house, the car, and Hopper's art collection, which was by then worth a fortune and was continuing to increase in value. But they agreed that Dennis keep his share of the profits from *Easy Rider*, that income from the film was not community property; Brooke didn't think it would make money anyway.

"I took a chance, man," Hopper said months later. "But I believe in the picture and it's going to give me my freedom—to make more like it, and to get out of cities. In L.A. the smog gets in your eyes. . . ."

CHAPTER SIX

Dennis went into *Easy Rider* grieving over his lost marriage but indignant that Brooke should have been so against the project. He failed to appreciate what hell he had given her in their six years together, how she considered his biker movies demeaning. When she had stormed out of the house taking their daughter, he expected her to come back, not go to an attorney. She was leaving him when he was about to achieve his lifelong ambition, directing. He saw it as betrayal. She didn't believe him when he insisted that it was not another biker movie, that it was a film that would show the violence underlying everything in America.

"The day I started the movie, Brooke said, 'You are going after fool's gold,' and that didn't read too well with me. Brooke is groovy, we even have a beautiful little girl, but you don't say that to me about something I've waited fifteen years—no, all my life—to do."

Hopper spent two years on the film, arranging the financing, working on the script, directing it, editing it for nine months, traveling the United States and the world with Peter Fonda and Jack Nicholson promoting it.

It was a moving account of young misfits crossing the Southwest on motorcycles. The beginning shows the protagonists, Wyatt (Peter Fonda) and Billy (Hopper), making a drug deal in Mexico. They transport cocaine across the border and collect $50,000 for it, which Wyatt places in a plastic tube inside his motorcycle gas tank. They decide to head east on their bikes, making for the Mardi Gras in New Orleans. The film chronicles their experiences in a series of encounters along the way.

At a small ranch where they stop to fix one of their bikes, they stay to eat a meal with the rancher and his Mexican wife and large brood of children. Wyatt tells the rancher he should be proud because "You do your own thing in your own time." After leaving the family behind, they pick up a hippie hitchhiking along the road. He brings them to the commune where he is the father figure.

At the commune they find some of the members bickering and others sowing seed on unplowed, sandy ground, but Wyatt, seemingly oblivious to the reality of their squalid situation, says to Billy, "They're gonna make it." Before they leave they have a brief encounter with two of the women from the commune. The four of them go skinny-dipping together.

Next they arrive in a small town in the midst of a patriotic parade. The long-haired bikers join the parade on their motorcycles and are jailed for parading without permits. The police are outraged by their scruffy appearance, especially Billy's shoulder-length locks and drooping mustache. Also in jail is George Hanson (Jack Nicholson), a liberal young lawyer, scion of a proper Southern family, whose alcoholic binges frequently land him in the lockup. Dissatisfied with his restricted life, George decides to join their trek to New Orleans. He looks forward to visiting a whorehouse there, which was highly recommended to him. That night they camp beneath the stars. They have no choice; whenever they drive up to a motel, the NO VACANCY light is quickly turned on.

When the trio stops to eat in a cafe the next day, the customers make mocking and threatening comments and the waitress refuses to wait on them. That night George tells Wyatt and Billy that people are certain to resent anyone who is free. After they are all sleeping, some men, presumably those that were in the cafe, attack them, killing George.

Wyatt and Billy go on to New Orleans. There, in a tribute to the memory of George, they go to the brothel he had so looked forward to. They pick up two prostitutes and go wandering through the streets, filled with the parades and Mardi Gras revelers. In a cemetery all four drop acid. The film shows their drug experience, represented in long, purposefully chaotic sequences of brief, often distorted glimpses of the characters and the cemetery.

Camped out in the night again after leaving New Orleans, Wyatt tells Billy, "We blew it." Billy doesn't understand—they still have their money, and they are still alive—but Wyatt does not explain. On the road the next day, two men in a pickup truck pull alongside Billy and point a shotgun at him. He gives them the finger and they shoot him. Wyatt tries to go for help, but the men overtake and shoot him. The last scene is of his bike flying off the rode in flames, burning by the side of the road.

Hopper wrote the screenplay with Peter Fonda and Terry Southern. A script was carefully completed before shooting, but the entire production would incorporate Dennis's fervent ideas about freedom of artistic expression.

"The script was left flexible enough that we could add to it or change it as we traveled," said Hopper. "Some things never changed. For instance, I knew that I wanted to use songs that were already popular, rather than a new score. I knew that Peter and I and the girls we meet would never be seen totally nude in the swimming scene, because I wanted to show the over-forty crowd that it is possible to play like innocent children in the nude without getting into sex. Even simple nudity would have killed the point.

"And I wanted to use actual residents of towns we went into, and let them say pretty much what they would actually say when they saw our long hair, and so on. I'd outline what I wanted in a scene, give them a few specific lines, and let them improvise from there. As for our characters, Peter's and mine, they were thoroughly set in advance."

Although neither Hopper nor Fonda will talk about it, there were problems in the production of *Easy Rider* in the early days, with Fonda considering calling off the movie. One report had Fonda carrying a gun and hiring a bodyguard to protect himself from Dennis. The clash was said to have come in the first weeks of production, when Dennis flew to New Orleans and started shooting without a script. The chaos was said to have grown faster than the film until Fonda stepped in and cooled down an overly enthused Hopper. It's said that he decked a cameraman who threw a television set at him, also that seventeen members of the company walked out. But whatever the case may have been, the movie went into production with the early difficulties swept under the rug and resolved.

The idea for the movie came out of the blue from Peter Fonda, who excitedly called Hopper in September 1967. Dennis immediately appreciated the concept for a modern Western using bikes instead of horses. Better still, the scenario was loaded with sociological messages that appealed to him.

Fonda recalls, "When I called Dennis with the story he said, 'That's terrific, man, what do you want to do with it?' I said, 'You direct, I'll produce, we'll both act. We can save some money that way.' I called him because I knew the genius (and I don't use that word lightly) he had and still has."

Hopper recalled the genesis of the project in these words: "Peter called me at, like, three A.M. and said he'd been sitting around getting stoned and playing his guitar and he'd had this idea. It was *Easy Rider*. Our real luck came when Bert Schneider and Bob Rafelson said they'd produce it. They gave us complete control. They just said, 'Go and do your thing and come back and show us.' And we did, man; except for the Mardi Gras scenes, we just started out on our bikes across the West and shot entirely in sequence, as things happened to us."

As director, Hopper made sure Fonda was the star of the movie. He didn't want anyone accusing him of using his first opportunity behind the camera to hog the limelight with his acting.

"It was important to me that Peter be the star," he says, "not because he's Peter Fonda, but because his character in the movie, Captain America, is the leader, good guy. You can't have a John Wayne without a Ward Bond, so I took upon my character [Billy, the spaced-out rebel] all the burden of explanation, the cynicism.

"Together we're symbols of this country today—Captain America, man, is today's leader—and when the small-town lawyer [Jack Nicholson] hooks up with us, you have a real American cross section. As we watch them we think of them as nice kids, but they're actually in their early thirties, an age when the establishment says they should be working, contributing. Instead, they're peddling dope. Because that seems no worse to them than the Wall Street tycoon spending eighty percent of his time cheating the government."

Hopper's hatred of redneck types comes into sharp focus at the end of the movie when his and Fonda's characters are murdered by truck-driving, rural, hippie-hating types who take their guns out of the rack and blast the long-haired, drug-soaked bikers.

In traveling across the country making *Rider*, reality imitated art. Hopper told an interviewer, "Every restaurant, man, every roadhouse we went in, there was a Marine sergeant, a football coach who started with, 'Look at the Commies, the queers, is it a boy or a girl?'

"We expected that. But the stories we heard along the way, man, true stories of kids getting their heads broken with clubs or slashed with rusty razor blades—rusty blades, man—just because they passed through towns with long hair.

"I went into one bar and immediately a guy swung at me, screaming, 'Get outta here, my son's in Vietnam,' and the local sheriff was right behind him, screaming that his son was in Vietnam, and I said, 'Now wait a minute,' that I was an actor and there with the movie, whereupon the boys' high-school counselor started screaming to get out, that his son was in Vietnam. And I thought, 'What if I was just traveling through and was thirsty?' So I said, 'Okay, I'm hitchhiking to the peace march,' whereupon eight guys jumped me."

Black movie writer and critic Michael St. John, who has interviewed Hopper and was also a friend of James Dean, explains, "Part of what Hopper was trying to say in *Easy Rider* is that young people should not be frightened to try and change America.

"Hopper told me, 'But if you're going to wear a badge, whether it's long hair, or a black skin, learn to protect yourselves. Go in groups, but go. When people understand that they can't tromp you down, maybe they'll start accepting you.'

"*Easy Rider* was a big statement for Hopper. Until he made it, he never really had a chance to express himself. The movies he made were the kind of movies he was fighting against.

"Hopper told me, 'Easy Rider shows the violence under-neath everything, how we talk freedom and democracy but can't bear anyone different from ourselves.

"'The motorcycles, those beautiful machines, in the movie really represent the American creation, but the two riders skimming across the country don't know what they're doing—they've blown it, really copped out.

"'Like their visit to the commune. The people are starving, someone has shot a horse for food, and Captain America keeps saying, "Beautiful, beautiful, they'll make it." He's got fifty thousand dollars in his gas tank—none of that is meant to be real, it's all symbolic even though motivations are cred-ible on a realistic level—but he never takes out five dollars to give to the people to buy food.

"'Captain America is Wyatt Earp, the sheriff riding the range; I'm Billy the Kid, representing the outlaw element. At the same time, whatever Captain America does is all right with me; I'd lay down my life for him. But the two riders never become involved; they're sick too, just like the estab-lishment. They won't take responsibility for what they see around them: They have the wrong goals, false values.'"

Hopper was still using drugs of one kind or another heavily during the time he was working on *Easy Rider*.

But he told British Broadcasting Corporation correspon-dent Barbra Paskin that what was unique about the way drugs were portrayed in the movie was that they were shown in a more realistic manner, in the context of the growing counter-culture.

"I mean, *Easy Rider* was the first time people smoked marijuana and didn't go out and kill a bunch of nurses or something," Hopper told Paskin. "They sat around and had a good time. It was the introduction of something. It was also the first time cocaine was ever smuggled in a motion picture.

"Cocaine was used and people had never heard of it. I was already using cocaine myself by this time, though in the movie we used baking soda. Suddenly at the end of 1969, at the beginning of 1970, cocaine was as common, if not more common, than heroin on the street. It was called the drug of kings before that. So suddenly, cocaine was introduced. Suddenly there were parties in Hollywood where everybody's going around with silver trays with marijuana on them and little things with cocaine on them. And it was sort of like everybody was out of the closet.

"*Easy Rider* wasn't a movie that pushed drugs, it was a movie that showed aspects of the drug culture that was catching on with the masses, rather than being the exclusive domain of so-called 'degenerates,' artists, and musicians. For years the 'in group' had smoked and done the stuff without anybody knowing."

He told another interviewer about what may have been his most memorable acid trip in the Sixties, the one he took with Jack Nicholson after shooting *Easy Rider* scenes in New Mexico.

"We'd finished our shooting in Taos, and we had a Sunday afternoon off, so Jack and I went up with some of the guys and we ended up taking acid at D. H. Lawrence's tomb. And we lay down in front of the grave . . . and then later that night Jack and I ended up with this beautiful young woman, and she took us up to a hot springs. And we were up there, naked, enjoying the water and so on, under a big full moon . . . and later Jack said, 'Let's run a little.' And so we had her drive the truck and we ran in front of the truck in the lights. And I remember Jack saying to me, 'We're geniuses, you know that? We're both geniuses. Isn't it great to be a genius?'"

Apparently the industry that had scoffed at Hopper for so long agreed with Nicholson. Dennis was suddenly being called a genius by a whole new generation of movie directors who were coming onto the scene at the end of the Sixties. *Easy Rider* was more than a countercultural phenomenon, so much so that it altered the economics of Hollywood production for some time afterward. It was made for less than $400,000 and grossed more than $50 million. It pulled in the youth audience that the big studios had not been able to attract. Hopper also had brought the film in on schedule and under budget. Coming on the heels of several $20 million, big-budget flops, the phenomenon shifted the studios' attention to small, interesting, risky productions. The brief brave new world of the "New Hollywood" was born—and Hopper was the nonchalant midwife. "My next picture is really going to be heavy, man," he promised friends.

Looking back on *Easy Rider*, it is impressive to see how well the film has held up as a statement about its time. When it was released in 1969 it was both propaganda and a phenomenon of pop culture. Years later it can be seen as a revealing sociological study of the 1960s counterculture. It documents the commune movement, the shallow nature of the hippie philosophy, the casual acceptance of drug use, and above all the quest for freedom, the freedom to "do your own thing."

While the beautiful photography of the Southwestern landscape and the bikes skimming along the highway celebrate that quest for freedom, the protagonists, Wyatt and Billy, are not glamorized into heroes. They are obviously flawed characters because of their hypocrisy. They spout flower-child maxims but have made their living from smuggling hard drugs—a career choice unacceptable to the love and peace crowd. This is underlined by the film's score when "The Pusher" is heard, with its bitter lyric: "Goddamn the pusher man."

As the main force behind the final shape of the film, Dennis displayed some interesting techniques that hinted at where he would go with his next film. One of the most interesting tricks was the use of flash-forwards. Instead of dissolving from one scene into another, flashes of the next scene were quickly intercut just before the previous one ends. For example, a night scene would be interrupted by a few momentary views of the next morning's scene before that next scene begins.

Before he got another chance to direct and show off his newfound directing technique—in fact, before *Easy Rider* was ready for release—Dennis spent a few weeks in the fall of 1968 as an actor on location in the mountains of Colorado. Henry Hathaway had come through with another job for Hopper. He had a small part, for a substantial salary, in *True Grit*, a John Wayne movie. Hathaway must have relied on the third time being a charm when he cast Hopper in the part of Moon, one of the villains of the film.

Besides the Duke, the stars of the film were young actress Kim Darby in one of her first feature films, country-western singer Glen Campbell in his first and last movie performance, and New York stage veteran Robert Duvall.

Campbell was enthusiastic to be making his first picture among such illustrious company, but Hopper and Duvall were not always as happy, though Dennis had learned to keep his ideas to himself around Hathaway. Duvall came to the set directly from the New York stage, where he was well known as an actor completely dedicated to his craft and with independent notions about working out character development on his own.

Hopper had already been lectured by Hathaway in no uncertain terms as to what was expected of him. If anything, he was more cooperative than he had been on *The Sons of Katie Elder*. He was learning that it was possible to follow direction and still maintain artistic integrity, working within the director's framework. Perhaps he had more empathy now that he had walked a few miles in the director's shoes.

Dennis later said he had learned something very important from Hathaway in the past. He told a reporter, "Henry Hathaway taught me a great lesson, a lesson I don't think I was able to accept until that point in my life, but one I've never forgotten. Don't fool around with the director! He's the man in charge and he gets what he wants. Just imagine what a mixture of styles and effects you would get if everyone was doing his own thing as an actor in a movie—what confusion! I love Henry now. I made *True Grit* for him and there's nothing I wouldn't do for him."

He watched with some amusement as Glen Campbell got a bawling out from Hathaway. An even better show came from the fireworks that developed between Hathaway and Duvall. Duvall had also watched Hathaway lay into Campbell and was prepared for more of the same. When the director gave him an order, Duvall blew up. According to some reports, a fierce row ensued.

Later Duvall said he did not appreciate Hathaway's method of directing; it was too much—as Hopper had once described it—"the old school marm approach," the director positioning each actor and telling him or her how to speak the lines. Duvall and Hathaway eventually resolved their differences enough to go on with the film, and privately Dennis sympathized with his fellow actor. He later had Duvall rolling with laughter when he recounted his run-in with Hathaway on *From Hell to Texas*.

By the end of 1969, Dennis was a completely reformed character in the eyes of Hollywood. He had acted well, and behaved himself, in *True Grit*. Moreover, he was a certifiable genius at making low-budget, highly profitable films. *Easy Rider* was opening the eyes of the movie moguls to a new generation of potential ticket buyers who wanted motion pictures they could relate to.

In the process of its success, *Easy Rider* polarized a new film audience of under-thirties, and generated a new school of talented young directors such as Nicholson, Peter Bogdanovich, Richard Rush, and Melvin Van Peebles. It established the style of the New Hollywood in which producers wore love beads instead of diamond rings and stickpins and blew grass instead of chomping on fat cigars.

Easy Rider wasn't, as Brooke Hayward had branded it, "fool's gold." Instead it was the mother lode, earning Hopper nearly $2 million. It also won the 1969 Cannes Film Festival award for the best movie by a new director. He was nominated along with the other writers for an Oscar for the screenplay.

In 1970 Dennis showed up at the Oscar ceremony wearing a western-style tuxedo, a Stetson on his head, and cowboy boots on his feet. He sat in the front row; at his side was Michelle Phillips, ex-wife of John Phillips, with whom she had sung in the Mamas and the Papas. More recently she had been going with Peter Fonda, but for now Hopper had her complete, adoring attention.

Dennis later recalled, "John Wayne was there. I remember seeing Elizabeth Taylor with Richard Burton; she was wearing a great big diamond. I hadn't seen her since we did *Giant* together."

It was the usual star-studded Academy affair, and in spite of his nonconformist apparel and outwardly rebellious attitude, Hopper was loving it. He was even glad to see the Duke walk away with the Oscar for Best Actor in *True Grit*. For Dennis personally, the night held some disappointment: He didn't win the award for the *Easy Rider* screenplay. But disappointment was tempered by the enjoyment of being back in the fold, among the celebrity faces seen all over the world that night. He said, "I didn't win, but I had a good time."

Having had a small taste of the high life, Dennis was ready to go back to work. He knew which story he wanted to put on film next. In fact, the script was already written. Now he had the clout to walk into a studio and have his terms met.

CHAPTER SEVEN

With the cash flooding in from *Easy Rider*, and the applause from an at-last-appreciative industry ringing in his ears, Hopper set out to make the movie that had been gnawing at his guts for six years: *The Last Movie*. He had written it in 1965 with another writer and they had signed Jason Robards as the star.

Record producer Phil Spector had agreed to put up the money but backed out at the last minute on the advice of an accountant, who said Hopper was too big a risk. None of the big studios would look at him at the time; his own wild behavior and the James Dean rebel legacy made him anathema to the "serious" producers.

In 1970 it was a different story; the Hollywood establishment, never slow to jump on a bandwagon, especially if it appeared loaded with gold, was making apologetic noises in the face of the honors and praise being heaped on Dennis's head. He was telling people *Easy Rider* was just a childish toddle in the direction he intended his future movies to take. If *Easy Rider* was a smash, wait until they saw *The Last Movie*. And he was going to bring it in for a mere $850,000, not the millions the majors routinely spent on features.

With this siren song playing in the background, he approached Universal, the studio that not too long before had brought America *Tammy and the Doctor* and *Ma and Pa Kettle at Waikiki*. They snapped up Dennis and his project, having had a taste of financial honey when they distributed *Easy Rider* for Fonda and Hopper. Nor did they worry unduly when he hired a cast that included some of the most conspicuous individualists in Hollywood, among them, Peter Fonda, Dean Stockwell, Jim Mitchum, Russ Tamblyn, John Phillip Law, and beautiful Michelle Phillips. He hired himself as the leading man and then invited everybody to a location fourteen thousand feet above sea level in the backlands of Peru, a country where all the major drugs—cocaine, speed, heroin, hallucinogens—were restricted, but some of them amazingly available and extremely cheap. Hollywood insiders were chuckling: Get all those cats together down there with Dennis Hopper and you'll have the wildest scene in the history of moviemaking.

Wild scene or not, what they didn't know was that management at Universal had cut a shrewd deal with Hopper. The contract said that he stayed in charge of the picture as long as he didn't exceed the budget and kept it on schedule. Dennis was only getting $500 a week for his work on the movie, but he'd get 50 percent of the profits. If it went over budget it came out of his profits; if he went over the million-dollar line he could lose all his share of profits. If he took more than the estimated four months on location, Universal had the right to send another director to replace Hopper. Under these stringent terms he got the total autonomy he demanded.

* * *

Peru had painfully learned to live with earthquakes, jungles, icy mountains, cannibalistic Indians, and deadly snakes. But Dennis Hopper was an entirely new peril. Even before he arrived on location he had the military government in an uproar. In Lima his first pronouncements were about marijuana, an illegal substance there, and homosexuality, equally taboo. He told a journalist from *La Prensa* that everybody should be "allowed to do his thing." He had blown grass for seventeen years. He had lived quite happily with a lesbian.

Nothing like this had ever before appeared in a Peruvian newspaper. When it hit the streets, the Catholic church was screaming and the ruling junta's colonels were howling with rage at the Yankee reprobate who found these vices "groovy." Within a day the junta denounced the article and was talking about a decree repealing freedom of the press. They investigated Dennis and their consulate in New York cabled back a description of a sullen renegade who talked revolution in his own country, a man who went to bed with groups, a hippie who had taken trips on everything that could be puffed, swallowed, or injected.

A thirty-eight-strong group of his cast and crew made matters worse with officialdom. They traveled on the plane together and as soon as the NO SMOKING sign was switched off, they were dragging on joints and getting drunk. They also "turned on" two stewardesses before they got to Lima. Passport control officials were soon making calls when this crazed group staggered into their country.

Additionally, Hopper and the movie had become a magnet to female groupies, who started arriving in Peru, attaching themselves to the set, and hanging out at bars where cast and crew drank. They had followed the company south from various points in the States to see the guru of new maverick directors work, to "join the big party." Dennis called them ding-a-lings, but was nevertheless involved at times with several of the girls he knew from the States. At first they weren't a problem and Hopper assumed they would eventually get bored and return home. But they didn't. Instead, they pursued the cast and crew, wandering from hotel room to hotel room, sleeping with anyone who would give them a bed for the night.

Peruvian officials held Dennis responsible for everything, including the welfare of a beautiful honey-skinned Peruvian girl who moved in with him after Michelle Phillips had finished her scenes and returned to the States. The lovely mestiza girl was observed shopping for marijuana and cocaine around Lima, presumably for Dennis. Soon after that Hopper got rid of the Peruvian girl, suspecting she was a spy for the Peruvian government. Dennis found there was very little he could hide from the authorities. The ruling colonels also put agents on the set who reported everything that was happening. Dennis was told to keep his cast and crew under control or they would all be kicked out of the country.

He told a friend at the time: "This shit don't bother me, man. It's the old establishment disapproval, man. Nothing to worry about, I got a picture to make, I got my art to express, and I'm going to have a good time, too. If they don't want to hear any more of my opinions, I just won't give any more interviews. Maybe that's the safest way to go until this film's in the can, till I'm back home and the colonels and their uptight country are history for me."

Hopper hadn't wanted to be in Peru in the first place. The original plan was to shoot the film in Mexico. But circumstances dictated that they be in Peru.

"At first I wanted to make *The Last Movie* in Mexico, but the government put too many obstacles in the way. Censors on the set, for the way the Indians were represented. They thought that we'd show too much reality about their poverty. Someone suggested Peru. I looked for locations all over and wasn't able to find the right one, although I found the country the most beautiful of any I have ever seen. I finally decided to visit the old Inca ruins at Machu Picchu and go home; then, in the office of the travel agency, I suddenly saw a picture with just the elements I wanted. A village of Indian farmers, a church on a big square, adobe huts, the peaks of the Andes in the distance. Chincheros was perfect! Every Sunday about twenty-five hundred people came to a big market; otherwise it's nothing but a hamlet with Indian farmers, shepherds, llamas, a rural area with striking scenery. Most of the Indians had never seen a movie: They didn't even know how to fire a pistol. Rifles, yes, but they had never seen handguns before."

In significant ways this picture was more important to Dennis than *Easy Rider*. While at the time he didn't admit it even to his closest friends, Hopper not only wanted this film to bring in the sort of money that would free him from financial worries for the rest of his life, but he also needed to prove to the industry that *Easy Rider* wasn't just a fluke—that he, Dennis Hopper, really did have consistent and growing talent. And this project was all Hopper's; he didn't have to share the glory or let Fonda take a larger share of the profits. Fonda had a small part in this movie but no ownership. In the case of *Easy Rider*, Dennis owned 7 percent of the gross while Fonda owned 12 percent. And on *Easy Rider* Fonda threw his weight about, complaining about locations, calling off shooting because he hadn't eaten. Dennis and he often had harsh words, came near to blows—especially after Fonda tried to cancel the picture in the beginning.

But everything was fine between Dennis and Peter on *The Last Movie*. Hopper said after the picture, "Peter behaved beautifully down there, man. I mean, better than he behaved on *Easy Rider*. I only needed him briefly at the beginning, he didn't have a big part. But he was beautiful, about things like showing up on time, and not crying about where he was, and not complaining about whether he had lunch or not, and calling off the shooting just because he hadn't eaten."

Dennis made a big impact everywhere he went, the locals marveling at this crazy Yankee. Visitors to the movie described him standing in the town square of Cuzco, the ancient, sun-bleached capital of the Incas high in the Peruvian Andes. He wore a cowboy's Stetson over shaggy brown hair, a crumpled chambray work shirt with a bandana, blue jeans, and scuffed boots, looking as if he had just climbed off his bike in *Easy Rider*.

The Indians stared with open mouths as the stranger, with red makeup spattered over his hands, tried to quiet a skittish horse while his cameraman waited for the right cloud formation to appear overhead. In his final week of shooting, after four months of work and play, Dennis's eyes were red-rimmed with fatigue and sleepless nights. His face was remote and brooding from the tensions of carrying this project on his shoulders.

Dennis told an interviewer at the time: "I got the idea for *The Last Movie* six years ago, but it wasn't until Peter Fonda and I made *Easy Rider*, that I could get anyone to put up the money. Then Universal said okay. *The Last Movie* is a study in responsibility. It's about a Hollywood movie company making a Western in a really remote Indian village. The movie company flies in and erects the false front of a Western street, the houses and the church, the saloon, all in front of the adobe huts where the Indians live. The camera rolls for the big scene: A pistol is fired at an actor who is standing in front of the camera. The Indians stand around, staring, unable to comprehend that what they see isn't really happening. Blood appears on the man's shirt as he clutches at his chest.

One Indian has to be restrained from ruining the shot by helping the man he thinks has been wounded. Then the director shouts 'Cut' and the actor gets up and takes off his bloody shirt. The Indians think they've seen a miracle. One snatches up the stained shirt and steals a gun; and after the company leaves, he constructs a camera out of sticks but he doesn't know the secret of the resurrection, of the miracle, and he tries to get one of the Hollywood crew who has remained behind to explain it. The movie explores the difference between various realities. The Indians associate the fake set with real prosperity brought by the movie company; even the priest eventually moves to the false church on the premise that if you can't beat them, join them.

"I'm playing the lead part myself. Originally I didn't want to, but after I tested a number of actors I finally decided it was easier to do it myself than explain to another actor what I wanted. In a sense, the movie is a structured improvisation; the script is there, but the dialogue has been changed and improvised by the actors to express their own approach. Each actor you cast subtly affects the whole by the way he reacts to situation or the way he gives his lines. My character, Kansas, stays behind when the company leaves because he wants to settle down in a little adobe hut, but he's taken over by phony dreams of building a big tourist hotel, an airport, even of building a ski run in an area where it never snows, of finding gold and making a million dollars, all corrupt dreams which turn his life into a lie. And then when he's finally finished, he asks, 'Why, why did all this happen to me?' We live on those dreams which don't have any relation to reality and they ruin our lives."

According to those who went to the Peruvian set of *The Last Movie*, Hopper looked quite different than he did during the making of *Easy Rider*. He had shed about thirty pounds of fat, which had been the result of swilling beer and eating junk food while on the road, and he had dropped at least a pound of hair, his long locks being cut back and his mustache shaved off. (Dennis, sentimentally, sent his trimmed-off hair in a box to his daughter as a gift, with a letter telling her to keep them for him and that her Daddy loved her.) In fact, apart from the cowboy clothes, Dennis looked almost establishment, his pale blue eyes glinting intently as he stared out at a cast and crew almost entirely consisting of friends and people who had worked with him on previous movies.

He would tell anyone who would listen that at last things were changing to his taste in the movie business. On one occasion he would tell a passenger in the jump seat of his chili-red truck, "Yes, man, the movies are coming out of a dark age. I mean, for forty years the uncreative people told the creative people what to do. But now we're telling them, like forget those big budgets. The only thing you can make with a big budget is a big, impersonal, dishonest movie. We want to make little, personal, honest movies. So we're all taking small salaries and gambling on a cut of the gross. And we're going to make groovy movies, man."

On another occasion, he would stop on a mountain track, roll a joint, take a couple of deep drags and give another perspective of filmmaking: "Ingmar Bergman is the greatest. He has it all together, man. . . . We think the Indians are primitive because they believe that hairy men come out of the mountains at night and carry off stragglers, but real people came out of the hills around L.A. and murdered Sharon Tate. . . . I see areas of light and shade first of all and color as an afterthought. Light is my obsession. I feel it as an elemental source of power, like a kind of cosmic coal. It makes things grow, it makes things die. It can turn into anything—a plant, an idea. Movies are made of light. Just think of the power of light to transform itself into everything we are and can imagine!"

Said an actor who worked on the movie in Peru, but who because of his continued friendship with Hopper did not want to be identified in this book:

74

"Everything Dennis did in Peru was groovy. He showed that he was willing to stick to his ideals. By that I mean he practiced what he preached: He was no Henry Hathaway directing by the rules, doing it by the numbers. It was an exciting and unusual experience of filmmaking. When he was behind the camera he was utterly absorbed, looking through the viewfinder after the cameraman set up the shot, framing the picture in his mind's eye. In front of the camera he was an actor really doing his thing, giving it all there was to give, he finished every day tired but happy. You could see that Dennis loved his work.

"But the problem at that stage of his career was that he was too deeply involved in alcohol and drugs. It distorted his perception, weakened the focus a director needs to put a coherent story up there on the screen. This was to become horribly evident later on.

"Dennis was a hard man to know at that point in his career. He was kind of hidden behind a veil of personal secrecy, although he was always making pronouncements about the world around him, always being rebellious and revolutionary, talking about people power and how it would eventually rule the world."

According to journalists who were on the set, Dennis was always a fascinating subject to interview but rarely let his guard down.

One reporter wrote, "Dennis Hopper had all the social skills—banter, earnestness, small talk, anecdotes, courtesy, command, shyness, anger, nonresponse—and he set them around his perimeter like land mines.

"All day he used them to control my approaches, my questions. He seemed afraid of something. I figured he was wary by disposition, wary of all close contact. I also suspected he was afraid I might distract him from his work, jab a leak in his emotional boiler just when he needed a full head of steam. He said a hundred thought-provoking things but allowed himself only one cry from the heart: 'Making things is agony. I hate to make movies. But I've got to do it. It justifies my existence. If I couldn't, I'd destroy myself.'"

Was the scene as wild as the pundits back in Hollywood had forecast it would be?

From the start Hopper was caught in the cross fire of local political problems. It happened in Chincheros, where the priest and the local Communist leader were at each other's throats. According to Hopper, the priest ground a fat living out of the poor campesinos and traveled abroad in style. When the Americans arrived, the priest sold them some roofing tiles that had been stacked in the village church. Next day the Communist leader accused the priest of selling community property. In a fury, the priest punched the Communist in the face. That set the women of the village screaming and cursing. They snatched up sticks and chased the priest across the village square hurling stones at him.

Displaying previously hidden diplomatic skill, Hopper requested a conference with the Communist boss and graciously made a second payment for the tiles. At the same time he mentioned that the road to Chinchero was pitted with potholes and washouts, making the drive over it in heavily laden trucks a perilous affair. The next day a quickly organized crew of Indians went to work on it, filling in the holes and getting rid of rocks that had tumbled onto the track. Hundreds of Indians lined the road as Dennis drove a tour of inspection. It was perfect. Hopper was so moved he cried. But it was wild personal stuff that made the set so crazy.

Life magazine's Brad Darrach was witness to some of the wilder, early days of location shooting in Peru. He described a morning in the hotel lobby shortly after his arrival. The thirty-foot-square room was packed with about forty actors, even more cabdrivers and bystanders, plus four members of the Peruvian civil guard, a general and a couple of bellboys. It was a scene of mass confusion until someone finally got through to the hotel manager that the friends Dennis Hopper had been waiting for had arrived.

Darrach described the group in the lobby: ". . . Russ Tamblyn turned up in cowboy boots and a full-grown Afro. Peter Fonda was wearing a colossal sheepskin coat, a small Bugs Bunny grin, and an ivory-handled .44 that once belonged to Tom Mix. Sylvia Miles, the bleached-blond prostitute in *Midnight Cowboy,* arrived in a dazzling chrome pantsuit that made her look like Milton Berle with breasts. Taking him for a bellboy, Sylvia ordered the Peruvian general to carry her bags upstairs. . . .

"By midafternoon the games became more serious. Somebody made a cocaine connection and a number of actors laid in a large supply at bargain prices—seven dollars for a packet that costs seventy dollars in the States. By 10 P.M. almost thirty members of the company were sniffing coke or had turned on with grass, acid, or speed. By midnight, much of the cast had drifted off to bed by twos and threes." Darrach went on to describe how his sleep was interrupted several times, once at 2 A.M. by screams he attributed to a young actress having a "bummer" trip on LSD and again at 3 A.M. by someone tapping on his window. It turned out to be a young woman he did not know standing on a wide ledge that ran the length of the building. Perched there in the rain wearing a drenched nightgown, she asked to come in when Darrach opened his window.

Darrach said that even wilder days followed. He reported that there was one group that enjoyed whipping parties and he claimed that one actor had chained a young lady to a porch post and, seeing something saintly in her posture, tried to reenact Joan of Arc's death scene by lighting a fire at the poor girl's feet. Darrach also reported another actor's close call with death when he took too many peyote buds at once.

The *Life* reporter tried to get a handle on why this talented group of young people felt the need to use drugs, and finally concluded that most of them used drugs because the others used drugs, that it was the thing to do in the hip New Hollywood. He added, "It's also the hip thing not to get addicted, but some of the people I saw in Peru were nibbling godawful close to the hook."

As time went on, local feeling built against the movie company. No matter what Hopper did to keep things cool, the resentment mounted.

According to Joseph Spielberg, an American who was studying and teaching anthropology at the University at Cuzco, there had been daily radio editorials attacking the film company. The most common complaint concerned the lack of respect shown for local customs and the insensibility of the company toward the problems of the people. Protests were made about natural settings being used without payment. The villagers claimed the crew had interfered with the performance of religious rituals. They felt that once again Peruvians had been exploited—this time by a wild group of perverts, Charles Manson look-alikes with beards and long hair.

But despite all the high jinks with drugs and booze, Hopper's achievements in Peru were not inconsiderable. He demonstrated an efficiency that few people who knew him expected. Consider only the elemental facts: Hopper and his crew shot more than two hundred thousand feet of film in just eight weeks. They persuaded their actors to work for small salaries and a percentage of the presumed profits. They kept the budget to $900,000. There were many extra expenses to contend with. For example, the unions required the production to keep union standbys for key crew personnel, because some of the crew members Hopper wanted weren't union members. Every member of the cast and crew suffered from diarrhea, from the cold and rain, and from altitude sickness. Chincheros, where most of the shooting took place, was almost twice as high as Mexico City, where the altitude had hampered athletes severely in the 1968 Olympics.

Governments and other institutions fought the production at every step. The FBI and CIA, according to Hopper and producer Paul Lewis, sent agents to check out the "hippie" filmmakers and their fondness for drugs. The Cuzco police reportedly stole the equipment for the horses that they had been asked to protect. The taxi drivers went on strike, complicating daily transportation to Chincheros. At the end of the trek, the truck drivers tried to hold up Lewis for more money. Though they had been paid for more days than they had worked, they saw their chance to refuse transportation when the plane was due to leave in one hour.

Although the first two weeks of production provided the later much-publicized freak show of partying and drug-taking, things settled down after that.

According to *Entertainment World* writer Winfred Blevins, who visited the set:

"Through all the difficulties, everyone seemed to work hard and well. Hopper's crew seems not only efficient, but essentially self-directing. Cinematographer Laszlo Kovacs, assistant cameraman Earle Clark, and gaffer Richmond Aguilar often managed between twenty and thirty setups a day, even working in a foot of mud during Peru's rainy season. They were working with an inexperienced assistant director, after Lewis fired the first assistant."

And according to *New York Times* reporter Alix Jeffry: "Hopper inspires something akin to idolatry in his actors, partly because he permits them tremendous freedom in interpreting their roles. Improvisation is definitely not frowned upon.

"Tomas Milian, a popular star of Italian films, puts it this way: 'There's something I admire so much in Dennis.

His brains, what he has inside of him, his personality, the contradictions. When I see Dennis, I see James Dean and I see Dean and I see Dennis. That is very strong.'

"One does get an eerie feeling watching Hopper. He wears Dean's ring at all times and when he rubs that ring he seems to become Dean. Seeing this happen, you feel a shiver suddenly creep up your spine. Everyone pretends not to notice, and in truth it is never mentioned."

The ring the *Times* writer referred to was a Mexican bronze and silver ring bearing the face of an idol. It once belonged to Dean and it came into Dennis's possession after Dean's death. It was given to him by a girl who got it from the lawyer who cleaned up Dean's house after he died.

And there was another strange story about that ring. During Lent, toward the end of the movie, the company was sleeping in an empty church near the town of Puno. One of the actors, Don Gordon, recalled that in the middle of the night he was awakened by weeping Indians who entered the church with lighted candles. The Indians stepped over the Americans in their sleeping bags, to pray before the altar. But Gordon, now fully awake, went outside. There he found Dennis staring up into the sky at a comet. Suddenly, eerily, the James Dean ring on his finger broke apart and the pieces fell to the ground. Dennis was very shaken by the fact that the ring had fallen apart. He took it to be a bad omen, a warning to get out of Peru before real disaster overtook his movie.

These feelings were heightened on the next-to-last day of shooting. Radio reports indicated the government of Peru might be about to fall. Producer Paul Lewis contemplated his government permits morosely. If the government fell, the permits wouldn't be worth the paper they were printed on. The crew wondered whether equipment and film might be taken, or if they themselves might be detained.

El Presidente maintained control, as it turned out. But

cast and crew fled Peru as fast as possible, before the government pulled more arrests out of its brass-buttoned hats. Before that, Hopper posed, bottle in hand, with the poncho-clad crew for a photograph for everyone's scrapbook. "The picture was not made on mahree-juana," he shouted gleefully. "This picture was made on Scotch and soda." Indeed, strong spirits had been a mainstay for the last three days, a hedge against the cold and altitude. As for marijuana, Dennis's personal supply had been stolen early in the production, so he had to bum grass from others who still had a stash for most of the movie.

Hopper brought back from Peru thirty-seven or thirty-eight hours of film. He had shot many scenes in several different ways, not knowing which he would use. Nor had he decided what the conclusion to the movie would be. But everything rested on his shoulders. He had total control of the final product, the final cut, the final edit, even advertising and publicity.

CHAPTER EIGHT

On his return from Peru, Dennis left Hollywood—much to the alarm of executives at Universal, who thought he would cut and edit *The Last Movie* in their own backyard at a location where they could safely and discreetly keep an eye on him and the progress he was making.

But it wasn't to be; Dennis went to Taos, New Mexico. Before he left, he commented: "The hardest part is yet to come. I mean, it's all hard, from getting the idea to putting it down on paper to getting people to act it out and so on and so on. But the editing—that's what I'm trying to resign myself to now, to spending five or six months with one other guy in a concrete cell chained to a machine. But I'm just one of those directors who happens to think a director isn't a director unless he does every little bit of his own editing."

When Dennis had first visited Taos during the filming of *Easy Rider*, it had been a magical time for him. This was the area where he and Jack Nicholson had tripped on LSD and had run by the light of truck headlights, celebrating their own genius. He was intrigued with one location he looked at but didn't use for the film, the adobe mansion that had belonged to Mabel Dodge Luhan, famed patroness of the arts, known for her support of English writer D. H. Lawrence during the last year of his life.

Hopper's first experience with his future home was supernatural: "I went to see the house when I was looking for places to shoot *Easy Rider*. It was a mystical experience; when it was time to leave, I couldn't get the door open to get out. Ghost-filled places have always fascinated me." He took the incident as a sign. "I'd been planning to buy a ranch in Elko, Nevada—a working ranch—but when I found out that Mrs. Luhan's granddaughter was willing to sell the house, I decided to go with the aesthetic-and-mud palace in contrast to the working ranch. I decided I was an aesthetic person and the other was a dream."

He abandoned plans to buy twenty-eight thousand acres of land in Nevada and instead purchased the rambling adobe structure near Taos. It was three feet from where the Taos Indian reservation began. The Luhan property included three structures. The big house had many rooms, each with its own door opening onto the central patio. There was a smaller house that Dennis would end up living in, leaving the larger residence for family, employees, and visitors. The third building was an open ramada, which was called the music house. Dennis filled it with percussion instruments for people to bang on.

He had traded his dream of a working ranch for a different dream. Now he fantasized of establishing a commune. The original plan called for a core of inhabitants to include Dennis and Michelle Phillips; Dennis's brother David with his wife, Charlotte, and their daughter; and other artists and artisans. They would have jobs in local businesses and live off their land. They would all love one another and coexist cooperatively. Apparently he had not been paying close enough attention to the lesson in communal living offered by *Easy Rider*, when the commune dwellers were starving and obliged to look for dead horses in winter for sustenance. Dennis thought he knew how to run utopia.

Soon after taking up residence in New Mexico, Hopper amazed everyone by turning his Peruvian fling with Michelle Phillips into a permanent relationship. As he confided to a friend, "Michelle and I are getting married because she just won't have it any other way." On October 31, 1970, they married in the living room of Hopper's adobe hacienda with 150 candles burning and Dennis reading aloud from the heretical Gospel of Thomas. Two hundred guests filled the hacienda to witness the couple exchange vows.

Shortly after the wedding, Michelle took off to join singer-songwriter Leonard Cohen as a backup singer, a gig Dennis later said he organized for his bride, to prove to her that they could successfully combine their respective careers with marriage. Eight days after the ceremony, Michelle called from Nashville, saying she didn't want to spend her youth in Taos, that she didn't like the scene Dennis was creating around himself, in short that she wasn't coming back. Her announcement shook Hopper, who was deeply in love with Michelle; he begged her to return.

As Dennis recounted it, "I wanted to show her that we could be married and she could still have her career. And we were married for eight days. She called me from Nashville and said, 'I'm not coming back. Music is my life.' I said, 'I love you, I need you. What am I going to do, I've been fixing up the new house for you.' And she said, 'Have you ever thought about suicide?' I paused for a moment and I said, 'No. Not really.' That was it. That's the simple truth."

The first crack in his dream of peaceful communal life was this second failed marriage. Dennis lost incentive to continue working on the main house. He had finished a room for Michelle's little girl, which the child never saw. The room remained untouched by anyone, the closed door a sullen memorial to the romantic tragedy.

After Michelle took off, Dennis was joined by his younger brother and five or six other people who formed the nucleus of his commune, working with Dennis editing the film, eating their meals with Hopper at the head of the table like their personal guru—as he was.

A frequent guest at the table was a stuntman, hired by Universal to act as Hopper's "bodyguard." Actually, the studio sent him to Taos to check on the progress Dennis made in the editing room and to report back. His bosses did not realize that Dennis had quickly corrupted his keeper and had him sometimes acting as a courier for drugs from L.A. on his frequent trips to Taos.

In the beginning, when Dennis was in residence all the time editing *The Last Movie*, the commune ran smoothly, mostly under the efficient direction of his secretary, Diane Schwab, aided by his sister-in-law. The place became a magnet for hip Hollywood types, stuntmen, actors, filmmakers, photographers, and journalists, so that the population on the ranch fluctuated from eight to twenty.

In addition to the ranch, Dennis had also bought a movie theater in Taos, where he tried to interest the local Hispanic population in entertainment such as films by Spanish surrealist director Luis Buñuel. He was puzzled and disappointed when the only show that could fill the movie house was a feature-length cartoon from the Disney studios. But he had not bought the theater as a money-making venture; it was to serve as a big screening room where he could run *The Last Movie* while working on it. Mostly, however, he worked on the film at home in his own editing facility.

With nearly forty hours of film to be cut down to a final two-hour product, Hopper was faced with an enormously complicated task, especially as he didn't know how to resolve many of the twists and turns of subplots he had shot spontaneously while in Peru. Much of that material ended up on the cutting room floor. But what Dennis did have was breathtaking photography, the skeleton of the original script, now on film—with many different variations of each sequence. He had shot four times as much film as the average director. But he had a principle to work from, and an ideally surrealistic background in which to set a parable of the real and unreal. Not caring about the screams of protest from Universal, his editing of the film was to take a year and four months rather than the six months studio executives expected.

With his assistants, Hopper would go into the editing room attached to his house at about 2 P.M. and not come out until 3 A.M. when, stoned, stumbling, and exhausted, he would tumble into bed. In the time he worked on editing *The Last Movie*, he could have put together three regular movies of the "biker" kind. But because there was so much riding on this film, he used the Peru footage in every conceivable way, varying the story, changing the ending, introducing subplots, making sociological comments about the plight of the Indians and the tyranny of the Peruvian junta. But work on the film didn't stop Hopper's bohemian way of life. Photographer-turned-documentary-filmmaker Lawrence Shiller spent eighteen days at the ranch in Taos co-directing with L. M. "Kit" Carson a documentary about Hopper as cult director cutting his movie. The scenes they got on film for *The American Dreamer* were amazing, to say the least. One was of their subject making love to two women in a bathtub; another scene showed Hopper in bed with eighteen young women in "a sensitivity encounter." While he claimed he was enhancing his creative abilities, others saw it as an excuse for having a good time with a bunch of naked teenyboppers. Whatever the motivation, it didn't stop Hopper from philosophizing. He spouted a lot of nonsense about free love, group unity, and individuals who had made life difficult for him.

According to another pal who visited him in Taos: "It almost seemed that Dennis had lost his mind; talking to him, it appeared that he was working on three different movies, not one. He was always changing the film, varying the message, striving for maximum impact. In the end I don't think Dennis really knew what he was doing. I've seen him come out of that editing room literally crying, begging for suggestions, then get furious with anyone who suggested an approach that varied from the one he'd decided on that day. I saw him with tears streaming down his face, I saw him drunk and stoned because of that movie. I thought that film was going to kill him, it meant so much to him.

"And when the bigwigs at Universal would call asking for a completion date he would go nuts. Dennis would curse them out on the phone, curse them out to his pals, then throw himself into another round of furious editing. None of us really thought he would finish the movie, we thought that he would have a nervous breakdown long before that."

After one year and four months in editing, *The Last Movie* was ready for showing. Even before its public screening, Dennis had a sense of foreboding, that he had produced something that only he truly understood. He dreaded hearing that his labor of love was not another *Easy Rider*. Nor did he want to contemplate his enemies crowing over his failure, saying he was a one-shot achiever.

He told an interviewer days before the movie had its first screening:

"It's a test for the audience—to see if there is that audience out there. I think people will have to see it twice before they understand it. That's a strange thing to ask people to

87

do if it isn't free. I'm not worried about it being a classic, and I'm not being pretentious by saying that.

"It *is* a classic. They keep saying classics don't sell, and art doesn't really make money. Art is dead, they say. It would be nice if that weren't true.

"In *The Last Movie* I show a little fancy footwork. I do all the things other movies do. I can make you laugh. I can make you cry. Where do we go now? It's a play. You can believe in it, if you want; people either love it or they hate it. . . ."

Most of them hated it. They felt Hopper had put them on, taken them for a gigantic ride. Even Hopper admitted to a writer that he expected the movie to make viewers feel "alienated, angry, confused, left out, cheated. . . ." And as he feared, they didn't understand the movie, but they certainly weren't going back to see it for a second time, as he thought might be necessary.

Pauline Kael, film critic for the prestigious *New Yorker* magazine, wrote:

> The directors of a few big hits have also become counter-culture heroes, and perhaps the most interesting question posed by Dennis Hopper's *The Last Movie* is not aesthetic but sociological: Is Hopper enough of a hero, because of *Easy Rider*, to get by with this movie? "Last" in the title appears to be used apocalyptically; I think Hopper means to say that there must be no more movies. He seems to have shot several epics. One is about an American film crew (with Sam Fuller as director and Hopper as stuntman) shooting a Western in the Andes of Peru; the natives imitate them and turn moviemaking into a ritual game—the camera is made of bamboo, but the bullets and bows are (maybe, we can't be sure) real.
>
> This epic also becomes a Passion movie, with Hopper as the Christ victim of the natives' game. (His

Christ looks like William F. Buckley gone hip.) Intercut is a story about a search for gold by Hopper and a buddy, and this story involves a profusion of native whores, plus some rich Americans, an amusingly hokey chanteuse, some sex exhibitions, and a very funny put-on about learning to find gold from the *Treasure of Sierra Madre.*

Straight and lampoon blur: is it a joke when Hopper turns into James Dean? I don't know, and I'm not sure he knows. Smashed together, the themes seem to form a gigantic classic paranoid fantasy, although that is clearly not what the director intended. He intercuts to destroy credibility, and throws in alternate scenes and occasional titles, such as "Scene Missing," so that viewers will not be able to sit back and be "carried away" by a story.

Finally, he fractures whatever seemed to be left of the themes. His deliberate disintegration of the story elements he has built up screams at us that, with so much horror in the world, he refuses to entertain us. It would be stupid to deny that there are reasons for screaming, but I doubt if Hopper knows what he wants to do, except not entertain us, and I'm afraid he will interpret the audience's exhaustion from his flailing about as apathy and complacency.

This knockabout tragedy is not a vision of the chaos in the world . . . but a reflection of his own confusion. Hopper as Christ is maybe partly put-on, but only partly; Hopper doesn't seem to have a face anymore, only a profile, and he can't take the camera off it.

The most embarrassing thing about his Christ bit is not that he has cast himself in the role, but that he has so little visual interest in anyone other than himself. The Peruvians in the film are an undifferentiated mass of stupid people; not a face stands out in the crowd scenes except Hopper's—the others are just part of the picturesque background to his suffering.

One would have to be playing Judas to the public

to advise anyone to go see the *The Last Movie*. Hopper may have the makings of a movie (perhaps more than one), but he blew it in the editing room. If he was deliberate in not involving the audience, the audience that is not involved doesn't care whether he was deliberate or not. That there's method in the madness doesn't help. The editing supplies so little in the way of pace or rhythm that this movie performs the astounding feat of dying on the screen in the first few minutes, before the credits come on.

Other critics pointed out that *Easy Rider* had been heavily indebted to the varied songs that changed the moods and rhythms. They lambasted Hopper for using lugubrious songs (the film score was by Kris Kristofferson) that dragged everything in *The Last Movie* to a standstill. While a few applauded his distinctive visual style, others urged him to get rid of the cutting room scissors and stop disrupting the flow of images in order to make stupid points about what's real and what isn't.

In general the critics tore Hopper's movie to pieces, calling it a self-indulgent piece of junk that simply was not worth spending good money to see. Ironically, *The Last Movie* had won an award at the Venice Film Festival.

This was the only upbeat aspect about the movie that Dennis had to cling to as he went on a short promotional tour that nearly broke his heart as he time and time again had to explain what was going on up on the screen. Even when he explained it to people, they didn't understand it.

"It's been no fun at all," Dennis admitted, subdued, pleasant in spite of it all, his somber face framed by shoulder-length hair kept in place by an Indian band. But he said, "I loved making personal appearances for *Easy Rider*, Peter Fonda and I must have hit ninety cities and everywhere everyone complimented us."

Dennis Hopper, a Hollywood newcomer
with big dreams for the future. (Ted
Lau/Photo Trends)

In this 1955 publicity shot, taken shortly
before the release of *Rebel Without a
Cause*, Dennis showed potential to be a
romantic leading man. (Pictorial Parade)

At the Hollywood premiere of *Giant*, with Natalie Wood, Dennis's brother David,
and Natalie's sister Lana. For the film's New York premiere, Dennis would defy
studio bosses and refuse to escort Natalie, showing up instead with a then unknown
actress—Joanne Woodward. (Darlene Hammond/Pictorial Parade)

Dennis with his first wife, Brooke Hayward. After their divorce he said she was "groovy" but her opposition to *Easy Rider* angered him. (Globe Photos)

Before his first blackballing, as Napoleon Bonaparte in *The Story of Mankind*. (Phototeque)

Hopper with his friend Peter Fonda, co-star and co-screenwriter of *Easy Rider*, in a scene from the movie. (Phototeque)

Dennis Hopper, a man of
many roles: cowboy,
pinstriped patron of the arts,
all-American football fan,
flower child. (Peter
Sorel/Globe Photos)

Dennis with Michelle
Phillips, arriving at the 1970
Academy Awards ceremony.
The following year they wed,
but the marriage lasted only
eight days. (Photo Trends)

In 1971, after the disappointing outcome of *The Last Movie*, Hopper waited in New Mexico for Hollywood to bring him work. (Manchete/Pictorial Parade)

The exile of Taos. (Manchete/Pictorial Parade)

With Daria Halprin, his third wife. Dennis drove her back to her family when his drug excesses became too much. (Globe Photos)

Hopper as Hurley, the manic photographer in *Apocalypse Now*. He was just as crazed off-camera. (Phototeque)

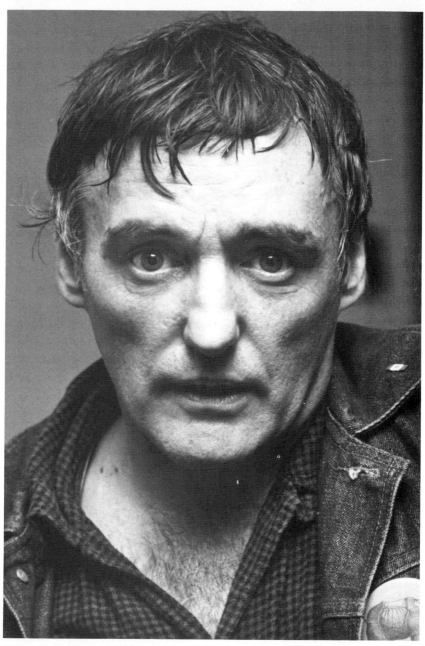

Hopper in 1980—seeing visions on his way to the bottom. (Ron Galella)

Passing the torch from one "Bad Boy" to the next—Sean Penn and a straight and sober Dennis Hopper. Penn was instrumental in getting Hopper his fourth directing assignment, *Colors*, starring Penn and Robert Duvall. (John Paschal/Celebrity Photo)

At the 1987 Golden Globe Awards with Maria Conchita Alonso, leading lady of *Colors*. He was nominated for Best Supporting Actor for his roles in *Blue Velvet* and *Hoosiers* but did not win. (AP/Wide World)

At the 1987 Academy Awards ceremony. The nomination for Best Supporting Actor for his performance in *Hoosiers* certified that he had made a phenomenal second comeback. Though he lost out to Michael Caine, he was happy just to be there. (Joe Bleeden/Globe Photos)

It was different this time around. Dennis Hopper was no longer a hero and everywhere he went he had to defend what was shaping up as the year's biggest bomb. Worse, doors that opened wide to him after his *Easy Rider* triumph slammed shut again, backers no longer standing in line to finance his next project.

The plain awful truth was that when he left Peru Dennis probably had a movie in one of the innumerable film cans that he brought home. But as Pauline Kael had said in *The New Yorker*, he had blown everything in the editing.

As a friend who visited him in Taos during the period pointed out: "What could you expect? He was doing all kinds of drugs, he was staying up late drinking with the boys and gals, he was roaring about the desert drunk and stoned. I don't think even Dennis knew what the story of *The Last Movie* was by the time he'd finished editing it. But despite all that, his talent still shone through."

There were those who understood what Hopper was trying to do in *The Last Movie*, and some who admired the work. They were prepared to usher him into the "auteur" school of filmmaking because he had stamped his second directing effort with the same distinctive personality that had shaped *Easy Rider*, using a similar style and reworking many of the themes of the earlier film. He had also demonstrated mastery of several film genres at once, among these the Western, the adventure movie, and most notably the movie about moviemaking, joining the tradition of Hollywood commenting on Hollywood, as seen in films such as *A Star Is Born*, *The Big Knife*, and *Sunset Boulevard*.

But even the praise-singers voiced cautions. Hopper had alienated the majority of moviegoers by overloading his film with religious and literary symbols and by using a nonlinear structure; it was just too difficult for most people to understand. On the other hand, the intelligentsia who recognized the symbols used and who were well-versed in contemporary artistic movements and themes would understand the film all too easily and ultimately find that it merely demonstrated the director's familiarity with these symbols and themes while failing to push that knowledge to a new level.

But the film was not bad, as so many critics informed the public. One of Hopper's champions was Foster Hirsch, a teacher of American drama at the New School and a contributor to *The New York Times*. He saw something in Dennis's work that was unique and brilliant. He writes:

> It is not, as most reviews lead you to believe, contemptible or vicious or idiotic: it is not a public offense; what's more it is not incoherent. It has temperament. Pace. Energy. Conviction. It certifies that the virtues of *Easy Rider* were not lucky guess work.
>
> . . . In his movie about moviemaking, Hopper mocks the phoniness of movies and their creators at the same time that he enshrines moviemaking in a mystique of glamour and adventure. *The Last Movie* is both a homage to, and a critique of, its own form.
>
> With the artificiality of moviemaking as its radical metaphor, *The Last Movie* is also a satire of the stereotypical American character: the obsessive materialism, the concern with surfaces, the urge to dominate. At this level, the film is a parable of the destruction of innocence, dramatized in terms of the intrusion of a rapacious, violent American culture on an eminently corruptible, equally violent primitive Peruvian culture. Additionally, the film contains a search, outside America, for the American Dream; it is a satire of the archetypal pattern of the Western; it is a modern Passion Play. For all the things it is (and tries to be), it is never a single-layered, unadventurous story of dopey Americans in an exotic culture.

Hirsch points out some parallels with *Easy Rider*. Kansas is "the rootless quester" just as Billy and Wyatt were. While

Billy and Wyatt "blow it" from the beginning of their quest, by making their freedom money dealing hard drugs, Kansas seems to have a chance to make his dream come true. The obstacle for Kansas to overcome in fulfilling his quest is himself: He is so completely a part of the culture he rejects that he can't help but bring it with him and it soils his dream. Instead of settling down to a truly simpler way of life in imitation of the Indians, he imposes an American-style house on a hillside next to a natural spring, sullying the pristine Peruvian landscape. He schemes about striking it rich, searching for Peruvian gold to plunder. Eventually, as Hirsch says, "Like the analogous character in *Easy Rider*, Kansas blows it."

Hirsch describes Kansas as a scapegoat for the sins of American filmmakers and capitalists. By staying in Peru after the rest of the film crew returns to the States and participating in the ritualistic games of the childlike but ultimately deadly natives who imitate the departed filmmakers by pretending to make a film about violence and death, Kansas carries on the role of martyr first mapped out by Hopper's character, Billy, in *Easy Rider*. As he is drawn further into the Indians' make-believe filming, he begins to confuse his role of The Dead Man with reality. In the end he takes on the guilt of his culture and is sacrificed by the Indians to expiate the sins of corruption and exploitation brought by Hollywood to the Andean village.

As the film concludes, the villagers, without fully realizing what they are doing, take their revenge against Hopper as a representative of the American materialism and decadence that has turned their existence upside down. The death of Billy the Kid in the Western is contrasted with Kansas's "crucifixion" at the hands of the Indians, and finally the director lets the audience in on the game he has been playing all along—that he is making a movie (*The Last Movie*) about making an imitation movie (the Indians' ritual) of a Hollywood movie (the Western). All pretense before the camera is abandoned; Hopper is seen outside his role as actor, even outside his function as director, as he makes faces at the camera to bring home his final point: It's a movie.

Foster Hirsch admits that the film is tricky, crowded, overly intellectualized. He also says that the narrative base can't comfortably support the superstructure crammed full with symbols and myths. But he maintains, "Nonetheless, Hopper has strived to erect a grander construction than most creators would dare," and the film "rightfully commands more respect and attention than it has received."

As the dust began to settle after the stampede of reviewers had trampled *The Last Movie*, Dennis was still fighting Universal to get the picture more widely released. They refused to do more than a limited release of a few weeks in New York, Los Angeles, and San Francisco.

Dennis said, "I didn't think the movie was going to be financially successful, but I thought it would be a classic. When the people at Universal saw the movie, they were horrified. They wanted me to recut it. I said no.

"They didn't want me to go to the Venice Film Festival with it, and they wouldn't allow it to be entered in the New York Film Festival. When it won a prize at Venice, they couldn't believe it.

"An executive said to me, 'We must have *bought* the prize for you.' But that prize was the only award given at Venice, and I won it, in competition with [Akira] Kurosawa, Bergman, and a lot of others.

"I don't respect anyone at Universal except Jules Stein, and he's not really in it anymore. Well, the movie's in their hands now, and their hands are full of blood—corporate blood."

Hopper said a Universal executive told him, "'Okay, so

you made an artistic film. What are we supposed to do, kill you? Only a dead artist makes money. We'll only make money on this picture if you die.' I said, 'Don't talk to me like that. You're talking to a paranoiac.'" Dennis was only beginning to feel paranoid—he could still joke about it. Years later paranoia would become a serious problem.

Studio executives tried to reason with the director to make changes that might salvage the movie's commercial viability. He later reported, "They said the film made fun of the movie business, and that business was bad enough as it was. And they wanted me to kill the guy at the end of the film; they didn't care how I killed him.

"Luckily, I had final cut. There were a lot of cigar ashes, speeches, screaming, pounding on desks . . . but they couldn't change the movie."

Dennis still considered himself an artist and laid claim to genius. At the same time he boasted of being basically illiterate, of having read "maybe eight or nine books" in his life. In spite of that he had picked up dribs and drabs of culture along the way, all of which he had tried to show off in *The Last Movie*. He had crammed it full of symbolic references to religion, legends of the American West such as Wyatt Earp and Billy the Kid, alongside literary legend D. H. Lawrence and pop icon James Dean.

If Hopper had an artistic vision to share with the audience, it was one he had borrowed from the abstract expressionist painters. He explained *The Last Movie* by saying, "In a way, it's like an abstract expressionist painting, where the guy shows the pencil lines, leaves some empty canvas, shows a brush stroke, lets a little drip come down and says, 'Yeah, I'm working with paint, canvas, and a pencil line.'

"Like the 'Scene Missing' flags are part of something you see every day while you're editing. So pretty soon you say, 'Hey, that's far out, 'cause I'm making a movie about movies, and that's another reality.' So I left them in—not only because scenes were missing, but also because it's something that brings people back to the reality of filmmaking."

The reality of filmmaking for Hopper was, for the time being, unemployment. He had no illusions about working for Universal again. He said, "Of course, I'll never do a movie for them again. I wouldn't want to do one for them anyway, but believe me, they ain't gonna ask me. They don't ever want to hear my name again."

And for a time the name of Dennis Hopper was not heard anywhere in Hollywood. He disappeared from the scene, into his own chosen exile in Taos. Occasional rumors floated back to either coast of wild goings-on at the adobe mansion, but most of Hollywood was pleased to let him ferment in the juice of his sour grapes.

CHAPTER NINE

Dennis Hopper's brief time as Hollywood's latest eight-day wonder ended in bitter self-exile in New Mexico. He took some consolation from the hard-edged beauty of the New Mexican landscape, the crystal-clear air, and the simple basics of life on the ranch. But he could not forget his disappointment about *The Last Movie*. He railed against the establishment's failure to recognize the genius displayed in that film. Resentful that he could no longer find financial backing to direct a movie, he cut himself off from Hollywood. Hopper retreated to the adobe in Taos, where he waited for them to come find him and ask him back to save the movies. From his drug-laden sanctuary he would occasionally emerge over the next twelve years to perform stunningly in little-seen films mostly made outside the United States.

There was a hole in him, Dennis felt, one he had tried to fill by using his creative genius to its maximum potential.

But now he had fewer outlets left for that creativity: He had abandoned painting after the Bel Air fire; he had thrown his cameras away when he directed *Easy Rider*; writing screenplays did not help if there was no chance of directing them, or even getting them produced with another director. So he looked elsewhere to fill the hole. Over the course of wasted years, he covered the globe seeking to wipe out the emptiness with acting, with women, with drugs, with drink, until he finally arrived at this last stop and discovered it was not within his power to obliterate the hollow feeling.

His disastrous eight-day marriage to Michelle Phillips and the failure of *The Last Movie* left him weary and defeated. He sought solace in drugs and booze, which he consumed in the shadow of his beloved Sangre de Cristo Mountains. However, the commune he had hoped to establish on the ranch failed to coalesce and the peace he sought at home eluded him through a series of misunderstandings between himself and the local inhabitants.

Dennis had exhausted himself defending *The Last Movie* in interviews with the press. Having suffered the scathing reviews given the motion picture, he felt reporters were hostile. He resented those who reviewed his life-style instead of his work.

He complained, "I don't know what trip the critics are on. Bad reviews are one thing, but don't review Dennis Hopper, the way Vincent Canby did. He called me 'a weekend mystic who drives to and from his retreat in a Jaguar.' Well, all I own is a four-wheel-drive Scout in New Mexico, and I'd like to run over him with it."

Nor did he understand how audiences could reject his latest effort when they had so loved *Easy Rider*. He asked, "Are audiences all that fickle now that they reject you after one film? All people seem to want is light sentimental stuff these days. They don't even care to identify with themselves anymore. The market is so confusing!"

Before he could completely cut his ties to Hollywood, Dennis had one more commitment to fulfill. He was to appear in a 20th Century-Fox comic Western originally titled *Dime Box*, which eventually reached theaters as *Kid Blue*. He had been signed to act in the film before the ill-fated release of *The Last Movie*. Prior to his departure for the location in Durango, Mexico, he deprecatingly described the movie: "It's apple pie, and ho, ho, ho. And the public will probably eat it up."

He played the antiheroic title character, an outlaw trying to go straight in the small Texas town of Dime Box at the turn of the century. The screenplay, written by Edwin Shrake, depicted a notorious outlaw-robber, Kid Blue, who tires of living on the run and decides to settle down. He chooses to start his new life in Dime Box, where the only industry is a factory that manufactures totally worthless ceramic doodads. The Kid is bullied by the sheriff (played by Ben Johnson), befriended by a factory worker (played by Warren Oates), and seduced by the worker's wife (Lee Purcell).

To earn a living, the Kid is forced to try his hand at polishing spitoons and wringing chicken necks before he finds a job on the assembly line at the ceramics factory, sticking American flags into bloblike ashtrays. The Kid's efforts to become a law-abiding citizen are viewed suspiciously by the townsfolk, and the sheriff voices their scepticism when he tells Kid Blue, "I seen boys like you before, and there's no good in ya." The sheriff launches a campaign of harassment against the former outlaw.

In the end, Kid Blue is fed up with the hassles and his unprofitable employment. He decides to go back to being the lawless kid everyone expects him to be. He concludes that the only way to save his pride and salvage his honor is to rob the fattest safe in town, and rides off into the sunset with his prize.

Hopper was playing himself again. He had tried to go

straight and work through the Hollywood system, just like Kid Blue tries to hold down an assembly line job at the Great American Ceramics Novelty Co., churning out ceramic ashtrays emblazoned with American flags. But that didn't work for Dennis because he wouldn't turn out little ceramic blobs of movies that were just like all the others; Dennis had to go back to the life he knew how to live, in the counterculture, as Kid Blue is forced to return to his criminal ways. Because the establishment, whether of Hollywood or of Dime Box, had labeled Hopper a rebel, Kid Blue an outlaw, neither one was allowed to take the place he wished for in society.

Like Kid Blue riding into the west with the contents of the safe, Dennis rode away from the film with $400,000 in the pockets of his dusty jeans—an amount the Hollywood press of the time called a "whopping salary, almost unheard of." The movie did not do well at the box office, and critics panned the film and complained that Hopper was getting a bit long in the tooth to play naive youngsters like Kid Blue. He looked thin and gaunt, aged beyond his thirty-six years. The cleanshaven look required by the role showed his sunken cheeks. He went back to his Taos retreat, in further search of himself, for the part he was missing that would fill the emptiness he felt.

When Dennis returned from the filming of *Kid Blue*, he realized he was surrounded by hangers-on at his commune. The people who lived there were contributing little or nothing to keep the place going. They functioned as drug-soaked sycophants, laughing uproariously at every comment of Dennis's, the ones he laughed at himself, funny or not, as they all hung out drinking beer, consuming peyote, and smoking marijuana, always encouraging Hopper to further indulge in drugs and drink. The higher he was, the less likely he was to notice how feeble their contributions to communal life were.

In late 1971 Dennis said, "I wanted it to be a commune, and we have had as many as twenty people, but now it's down to four or five. We've been going through a lot of changes. I just threw a lot of people out of the house in the last couple of days. There were a lot of freeloaders. When I was here for a year editing the movie, we had it all together, but when I left and came back again, it had become a playground. People were very undisciplined. Originally, I hoped everybody would get involved in community business, but there's no work here, no jobs, nothing for them to do. All the communes in the area are full, and most of them have to work very hard just to get their food."

The other communes he mentioned numbered no less than thirty when Hopper first moved to Taos. The population of hippies preached flower power and love, but instead animosity blossomed between them and the local inhabitants. Dennis arrived on the scene looking like another hippie, with his long hair and headband, his jeans and love beads. The look was hippie but his attitude was more like the Lone Ranger. He was there to bring justice to the persecuted and misunderstood—his people.

Talking to a visiting journalist, Dennis tried to explain the atmosphere around Taos. He said, "The area is predominantly Spanish and Indian. I had a lot of trouble at first from the local Spanish, who didn't want to see an influx of Anglos, especially hippies. Most of the residents live on about eight hundred dollars a year, eighty-five percent of the land around here belongs to the government, and there's a lot of violence. Not abstract violence, like the violence in big cities, where you read about it in the paper. Out here, when somebody gets shot, you know the person who got shot, you know the guy who shot him, and you know why he shot him."

Not long after they had passed, he recalled the early days of his life in Taos: "It was bad when I came here, man, really bad. Suddenly there was me, this movie freak, with my brother and all these hippies around, and the locals didn't dig it. Every time David and I would walk into town these cars would come swinging around us with guys leaning out yelling, 'Hey, man, we're gonna rape your wife and your sister!' Hippies would be hitchhiking and when the cops spotted them, they'd call the high-school football team and those guys would come beat the shit out of them—while the cops were watching! After a while, the cops'd blow their sirens, and when the high-school kids had disappeared, they'd arrest the hippies. And the guys were getting mutilated and the girls raped.

"Finally one night I said, 'Fuck it,' and got a gun and put it in the backseat of the car. So sure enough, a bunch of kids stopped me and my brother, like they were going to ask directions. I got out with the gun and said, 'Okay, everybody up against the wall.' I'd seen too many John Wayne movies."

The showdown in Taos went on: "I made a citizen's arrest and held them all at gunpoint until the cops arrived. By the time David had called the police, there was a lynch mob out there of a good hundred and fifty people wantin' to hang our asses. It looked like a scene out of *Viva Zapata*—pitchforks, machetes, the works."

To Dennis's dismay, the police arrested him and David instead of taking in the locals he had been holding at gunpoint. Bail was eight thousand dollars. "When we posted bail, the police said, 'We're going to let you out a side door. We can't protect you, because of the lynch situation.' There were sixty or eighty farmers still outside, and then five guys just back from Vietnam came in and told me, 'We're going to kill you.' I pointed out to the police that I'd just been threatened. 'Shut up,' they said."

Not content to have stirred up a lynch mob, Dennis escalated his campaign. He made some calls to gather his "gang" together; it was time to prepare for a shootout. "I called some stunt men buddies of mine in Hollywood and said, 'Look, I need your help, 'cause the police sure aren't gonna help me.'" The next day he went into a local sporting goods store where he said he and David bought up every gun in the place.

Reinforcements rode to the rescue from Hollywood; his stuntmen buddies showed up. Dennis continued his tale: "We set up machine-gun nests and rifles on the rooftops— good fields of fire. Then David and I went to the high school and we burst in on their assembly. We had guns hidden under our ponchos. I was up on the stage and David in the back. I told the kids, 'Look, I'm here and here I'm going to stay. What's more, there are more freaks coming in over the next few months, and though they may have long hair, they are not the love generation. They're back from Vietnam, and they're hard dudes. They will have weapons—like these.'" Dennis and David whipped their ponchos aside for a moment to flash their automatic weapons at the astonished assembly. "'Macho is macho,' I explained to them, 'and if this keeps up, somebody is going to get hurt around here. Just because these hippies are dropping acid, that doesn't give you the right to rape their women and cut their balls off.' Well, they listened, and they finally got the message."

Dennis followed this performance up with positive community involvement, trying to mollify the main elements of the community. He paid for the Teatro Campesino, a traveling Chicano theatrical troupe, to come to town and perform, and he worked on behalf of the local Indians in their effort to get back some of their land in the Blue Lake area. Hopper and his people had no more trouble with the local citizens. As Dennis put it, "Once they decide you are macho, they leave you alone."

Dennis had not endeared himself to the local authorities, however. They kept a watchful eye on him whenever he came to town. The police later arrested him again for possession of a deadly weapon—they stopped him in the main plaza of Taos carrying a loaded .357 Magnum revolver. By the time he stood in front of the municipal court judge, Dennis faced one count of disorderly conduct, two counts of verbal assault, and one count of resisting arrest, in addition to the weapon charge. He pled guilty to all charges and the judge let him off with a mere three-hundred-dollar fine. Just a month before that he had been involved in a motoring accident and been fined three hundred dollars by the same judge for leaving the scene of an accident and failing to report it. All of these incidents were dutifully reported by the Hollywood trade paper *Variety*, adding to Hopper's wild-man legend with the film industry.

He went on to shock the good citizens of New Mexico with his testimony before their state representatives. In Santa Fe, the capital, Dennis testified before the state legislature's Drug Abuse Study Committee. He made an impassioned plea for legalizing the free use of marijuana. He told the lawmakers, "Marijuana will have to be legalized because you can't keep making criminals out of the majority of our citizens. Otherwise the country will fall apart." He followed that plea with statements that were anathema to the assembled politicians. He advocated legalizing the medically controlled use of heroin by confirmed addicts. He claimed it would be a major advance in stopping the wave of crimes committed by addicts. He warned that society should be especially concerned about the increase in addiction to hard drugs among veterans returning from Vietnam.

Dennis boldly persisted in publicly linking himself to illegal drug use, though he denied his own use of heroin or other "hard" drugs. He once told a reporter, "I was never on hard drugs at all. Hell, if anything, alcohol is my addiction." Yet a few years later he would tell another interviewer about his preparation for doing a movie of the William Burroughs novel *Junkie*. He, his friend Terry Southern, and novelist

104

Burroughs all worked on several screenplays for the film that was never made. He said, "There was a year that we were together in New York, in the late Seventies. I got to spend a lot of time with Bill; he's an incredible man. [The movie] was never made. I did a lot of experimentation with heroin at that time."

Dennis was seldom seen without a beer in one hand and a Marlboro cigarette burning in the other. Visiting members of the press reported that pot and peyote were passed around freely. If he tired of beer, Dennis would go for a martini, a Scotch and soda, or rum. He recalled how his drinking habits had changed when he left San Diego as a young man: "When I got to Hollywood, I was strictly a beer kid, but they were all drinking martinis. At first, I thought the stuff tasted awful. It's an acquired taste; I acquired it."

He especially needed the heavy stuff on his infrequent forays to either coast, to show the film industry he was still alive. He said of this time, "To tell the truth, it's just plain difficult for me to be in society—to be a social being. That's why I'm better off up here, in Taos. New York and Hollywood are hard for me, where you have to go and sit in a producer's lap at those parties. Oh, I can do it for a while, but then I find I'm acting. I think it's my worst performance. I try to be polite and courteous, and then, sure enough, I get pissed off and blow it. Let's face it, I can't stay on my best behavior for long."

He was up to his old tricks. "At parties I'd nail a producer in a corner and demand to know, 'Why am I not directing? Why am I not acting?' Who wants to deal with a maniac like that?" At this point, no producer or director in America did.

In 1972 his public statements were laced with bitterness. He would tell people, "I got nothing coming up. I got nothing, man. I'm a failure. I'm out on the street again." At the end of that year he was on the publicity trail again, ironically to promote the rerelease of *Easy Rider*. His continuing participation in the profits from that film made it worth his while to cooperate with Universal's promotion efforts. For the time being that movie looked like his only sure source of income.

He still could not find financing for another film of his own. He had wanted to make another motion picture with Peter Fonda, called *Second Chance*, based on their experiences in New York when they were seeking backers for *Easy Rider*. He would eagerly describe the movie he had in mind: "The way the picture begins, Peter and I are driving to the airport in L.A. to start the trip and I'm saying, 'We've got to save the movie industry, man. We gotta save it, or it's all over for the movies!' That's what the picture is about." But Dennis had already used his second chance; now Hollywood turned its back and went in search of other saviors.

Dennis stayed in Taos seeking something other than the money and fame valued in Tinseltown. A mystical aura surrounded the place he had chosen to live. There were sacred Indian lands in the foothills of the Sangre de Cristo Mountains. The reservation began just a few feet from the door of Hopper's adobe mansion. The area was also sacred to a sect of fanatical Catholic Hispanics called the Penitentes who were rumored to reenact the passion of Christ each Easter by actually crucifying one of their members.

He was drawn to the mountains; he said it was the first place he had felt at home. He was also drawn to every local legend, supernatural rumor, and shred of mysticism he ran across. He began collecting bits of belief systems the way he collected art, pulling together an eclectic mixture consisting of pieces of varying value. He took what he understood of Indian spiritual ways: "It's like, a rock is a rock, a mountain is a mountain, water is water. . . ." He combined that with unusual beliefs about the healing power of metals. Speaking of the copper ore in the Taos area he said, "It has the highest ion count of any in this hemisphere, second only to Tibet, and if you drilled through the Earth right now you'd reach Tibet; it's like the brains of the Earth. But the copper is causing an overreaction and it's pulling the poison out of me." He thought it might help him live to be a hundred years old, if he could only make it past his next birthday.

Into this mix he threw what he had gleaned from the *Gospel According to Thomas*, a book given to him by a black prostitute in the lobby of a New York hotel. He recalled how he was introduced to the teachings in 1969 and paraphrased the apocryphal religious text: "I was an atheist at that point, and it was pretty far out. We read it aloud, and I couldn't find anything in it I couldn't believe. I take it literally, although it's sort of a puzzle. It's an evolutionary, revolutionary document—part of the Dead Sea Scrolls. 'If you don't dislike what's going on, then you're not involved,' it says. It is not for a church. 'When you are one or two, I'm with you. When there's more, you become as gods, and you better behave as gods.' It says, 'Don't lie, and don't do what you hate, and all the secret wonders will be revealed to you.' I don't lie, and there really are miracles as a result. Lying becomes a way of life for people, and moves into every area. If you stop lying to yourself, you stop lying to others. You lose a few friends, of course. But you can see things other people aren't seeing; it makes it easier to see the miracles of life."

The combination of drugs, alcohol, and mysticism began to work on Dennis until his visions were more frightening than miraculous. He was seeing things at night, when the substances he had consumed were still fighting it out in his body and wouldn't let him sleep. He had preferred to believe the local legend that writer D. H. Lawrence, who had spent his final days as Mabel Dodge Luhan's guest, was buried in the courtyard of his home and not up in the cemetery. It seemed romantic at first. But then he started seeing what he thought was Lawrence's ghost wandering across the patio.

A friend who was an occasional visitor to Taos recalled Dennis's behavior there: "He was in a paranoid state there—totally confused. He saw things, he started imagining things. His imagination started taking over where he was seeing images and he thought they were for real—seeing ghosts and stuff. He thought he was losing his mind at some periods."

There was another shade that sometimes haunted his sleepless nights. This one was younger, a thin blond young man in his early twenties. Why did he look so young now? Dennis wondered. He used to look up to him as the older and wiser one. Now he looked like such a young kid, it made Dennis feel like an old man. Dennis called out, "Jimmy! Jimmy, is it you?" The vision would fade, but it left behind reminders of all those youthful dreams. He wondered how he had come so close to fulfilling them, only to watch them recede into the distance once more.

Dennis met a young woman he thought could help fill some of the empty space in his life. Daria Halprin was a dark, sensuous beauty who had begun a film-acting career almost by chance. She had been spotted by avant-garde Italian director Michelangelo Antonioni (most famous for his film *Blow Up*). Antonioni cast Daria as leading lady in his first picture filmed in American, *Zabriskie Point*, a movie that Foster Hirsch had compared to Dennis's own *The Last Movie*. For a time Daria was a darling of the art scene, where her path soon crossed Hopper's. It was not long before they were completely wrapped up in each other and Dennis was ready to take the marital plunge for the third time. Daria was so enthralled with Dennis she couldn't hear the horrified protests of her traditional Jewish family. They were upset at the prospect of an aging hippie groom who barely believed in anything Christian from what they could make out, let alone Judaism.

However, in 1972, with her family's acceptance of Dennis and to the amazement of Hopper's friends, he and Daria married in an outdoor ceremony at a spot overlooking San Francisco Bay and the Golden Gate Bridge, near her parents' home. The rabbi was there to perform a traditional Jewish ceremony, but there was little else familiar about the event. The fifty-five guests there to witness the offbeat nuptials were signaled by a trumpet blast to climb the hillside and take their seats. While waiting for the bride to appear, they listened to a composition for synthesizer, ram's horn, flute, and Yemenite trumpet, recorded especially for the wedding. Daria, dressed in a purple velvet Navajo dress, joined her long-haired groom, also dressed in velvet, beneath the bridal canopy designed by her father, a landscape architect. As the ceremony came to its close, Dennis dramatically raised his foot and performed the traditional crushing of the glass beneath his snakeskin cowboy boot. At the reception the bridal party danced Jewish folk dances to the beat of a conga drum.

Dennis returned to Taos with his new bride. Daria's acting career until then consisted of two movie appearances. Her brief flirtation with fame had begun with her debut as the star of *Zabriskie Point*, released in 1970. That film had stirred some controversy over a nude love scene in which Daria and her co-star had made love in the desert surrounded by dozens of other writhing groups of twos and threes in various stages of undress. The motion picture had more notoriety than popularity and Daria herself was described by the *New York Times* critic Vincent Canby as being "a sweet aimless girl who runs flat-footedly" when he included *Zabriskie Point* in his choice of the ten worst films of 1970. Daria finished off her film career in a forgettable thriller called *The Jerusalem File* in which she played a beautiful Israeli student activist torn by her love for two men.

Dennis was not going to make the same mistake with Daria as he had made with Michelle Phillips. He would keep her with him. If she was going to do any more acting, it would be in his films. He was all set up for moviemaking in Taos. As soon as someone got ready for him to make a picture, he was prepared. He had the facilities right there at his home. Right on his property he had the big house for guests and employees to live in. He and Daria were living in the smaller house. He had the editing room set up and the theater in Taos where he had installed a synch sound system. He had his loyal friends he knew he could call on for actors and crew as soon as he needed them. He still had plenty of script ideas that he thought would make dynamite movies if he was just given the chance. For a while he believed that if he just held out long enough in Taos, the opportunities would come.

As he much later told a reporter, "I said, 'Well, they should be bringing me movies, I mean I'm, you know, a genius.' I mean, I'd bought a theater where I had synch sound, I had all my editing equipment, a big complex where everybody could live. . . . I had no product, I had nothing to make. I didn't go back [to Hollywood]. I wasn't visible. . . . And I'd get crazier and crazier because I wasn't working and I wasn't doing the things I wanted.

"I would work, I'd go off and act, I'd do films in Europe and all over the place, but I, you know, I never went back. Saying, 'They've got it against me.' And it was all bull.

"Because it was me. It wasn't Hollywood. Okay? It was me. It wasn't the industry. The industry was going along doing fine. It was me."

Not surprisingly, there was no line of movie executives banging on the door to his adobe, waving offers to finance another Hopper effort. Gone were the days when a director like Henry Hathaway would take another chance on him. The rumors that were getting back to Hollywood, via the visitors to the ranch, told of an increasingly insane and drugged-out hippie. Instead of mellowing with age, reports indicated he was more rebellious than ever. When people heard Hopper's tales of confrontation with the law, they were not sure whether to give credence to it all, but one thing was evident: Hopper believed every word of his own legend. No one doubted that he was capable of any bizarre behavior he laid claim to.

For young Daria, the seclusion of Taos was the kiss of death to her acting career. Soon she was the mother of a baby girl that she and Dennis named Ruthana. She dedicated herself to being a mother and wife, though she was increasingly disturbed by her husband's sudden mood changes. She worried about his fascination with guns. Being a city girl, she wasn't sure how unusual it was when Dennis killed a pig with his .22 pistol, then covered it with shaving cream to shave the hair off.

If anyone in Hollywood still remembered Daria Halprin, it was to recall that she had married that crazy man, Dennis Hopper, and to wonder what became of her after that.

Dennis was remembered, but not when it came to offers to work in establishment films anymore. But other young maverick directors remembered him. They were working outside the Hollywood studio system. That gave them the freedom to hire people who were not acceptable to mainstream movie moguls. Some were friends who still believed in Dennis. He began to work as an actor again.

CHAPTER TEN

The mid-1970s was Hopper's time to prove himself as an actor. He worked whenever he could, starting with starring roles in small films. The first of those, *Tracks*, sat on the shelf for four years before it was distributed for theatrical release. In the meantime, by the middle of the decade Dennis was captured for the screen in three outstanding performances in three very different movies: *Mad Dog Morgan*, *Apocalypse Now*, and *The American Friend*. But these opportunities to hone his acting skills did not assuage his burning ambition to direct. His bitterness over *The Last Movie* did not fade with time.

His career reached an artistic high by 1977 with three great performances behind him, but by the end of the decade too few people had seen those films and Dennis was reduced to the status of supporting player to newcomers in low-budget films. Between acting expeditions to Australia, Europe, the Philippines, and Mexico, he fled back to his refuge in the shadow of the Sangre de Cristo Mountains, where he awaited word that Hollywood wanted him back.

That refuge sometimes felt like a trap, especially when there was no money coming in. His third marriage was breaking apart under the pressures of isolation in Taos and Dennis's drug-induced personality changes. Years later he would grieve over his third marital split, saying, "If I hadn't gotten on drugs, I'd be married to her today." When Daria left him for good, she took Ruthana with her and for a time went back to her family in San Francisco.

Dennis took work whenever it was offered, but it was offered infrequently. In 1974 he jumped at the lead in a film written and directed by a friend, Henry Jaglom. The film, called *Tracks*, was Jaglom's attempt to dramatize his intellectual and moral outrage against American involvement in Vietnam. The philosophy of the movie appealed to the actor; he had held strong anti–Vietnam War views and had often voiced them, much to the disgust of Jay Hopper, his World War II veteran father.

Dennis starred as Army Sergeant Jack Falen. Back from the war, he escorts the body of his dead war buddy home for burial on a cross-country train ride. Also in the cast was Hopper's old friend Dean Stockwell, a burnt-out child actor who had dropped out of the Hollywood scene and was now resurfacing in the offerings of counterculture directors like Hopper and Jaglom. Stockwell played an aging hippie also traveling on the train. The role of another passenger, a naive and decent college girl, was enacted by Taryn Power, daughter of screen legend Tyrone Power.

The movie consisted of a plotless series of vignettes in which Sgt. Falen meets a cross section of America on his transcontinental trip, which takes place at the time President Nixon was announcing the signing of a cease-fire to end the war.

Dennis felt nothing but frustration when, after working

hard on the film, Jaglom could not find a distributor for it. For several years the picture surfaced occasionally at film festivals around the world. Dennis felt he had done some great acting in the picture, but when *Tracks* finally had its theatrical release in 1979, the critics disagreed with Hopper's self-assessment. Blame for the film's failings was meted out equally to Jaglom and Hopper. One critic called it "an inarticulate flower movie" and went on to say, "The mechanics of Mr. Hopper's performance are so apparent they subvert the film's claims to serious purpose and turn it into a cross-country ego trip."

Hopper's career was sliding fast toward oblivion. He pestered his agent for work. There were some offers, but they were for unsympathetic roles in foreign films. Dennis was advised to turn down certain offers because the characters lacked "redeeming qualities." "This is a phrase I've heard throughout my career," Hopper would later say. "Especially when my bank said 'empty.' I heard, 'This character has no redeemable qualities.' And I said, 'It sounds redeeming to me. Do they pay money?'"

Assured of monetary reward, Dennis took off for "the land down under" in 1975 to work on *Mad Dog Morgan*, an Australian film released in the United States in 1976 under the title *Mad Dog*.

His part was that of Irish-born criminal Daniel Morgan, who terrorized Australia during the mid-1800s. The film was directed in Australia by London-based director Philippe Mora, from his own screenplay. Dennis saw plenty of redeeming qualities to the assignment besides the money. It was a challenge that would contribute to his growth as an actor. He practiced with a dialect coach until he perfected an Irish brogue for the role. Critics would later praise the richness of his accent. His co-stars were some fine Australian actors: Jack Thompson as the policeman who tracks Morgan, David Gulpilil as Morgan's aborigine accomplice, and Frank Thring as a dastardly police superintendent.

The story was set in Australia of the 1850s, a time when the country was still making the painful transition from being Great Britain's penal colony to being a full-fledged nation. At the same time, there was a gold rush that attracted every manner of adventurous fortune hunter. Among the wealth-seekers is Daniel Morgan, Hopper's character. In the gold fields Morgan one day attacks a bully who has been persecuting a Chinese man. Morgan's punishment is swift. He is sentenced to twelve years at hard labor, the type of sentence that assured a continued supply of cheap labor for building Australia's highways. His first two years are served locked in irons.

In prison, Morgan is branded and gang-raped. He takes out his rage in his work, breaking rocks and chopping trees with such zeal that his sentence is reduced to six years. The hellish prison experiences, however, have left Morgan insane with rage, ready to seek revenge on society. He becomes a latter-day Robin Hood, robbing the rich to help the poor and making fools of the authorities he so easily eludes with support from the impoverished, oppressed people who make him their hero—much as Jesse James and other outlaws of the American West gained hero status in the chaotic aftermath of the U.S. Civil War.

Hopper exquisitely played out the contrasting madness of the criminal against the sometimes childlike naiveté of the man who probably would have preferred to be a member of the ordered society he rampaged against, had circumstances allowed. The actor gave life to the legendary Mad Dog, considered scarcely human by his contemporaries, roaring across the Australian bush with long hair streaming and pistols blazing. While obsessed with nurturing his own myth and proud of the thousand-pound reward price on his head, Morgan becomes paranoid that even those he has trusted will turn him in when greed gets the better of them. At the film's end, law and order prevail. Mad Dog is tracked down and killed, his dying words lost in a gurgle of gushing blood. The police superintendent has the final word, requesting the criminal's scrotum to be made into a tobacco pouch.

Mad Dog Morgan went to the marketplace at the Cannes Film Festival where it was picked up by a distributor for American release, unusual for an Australian film in 1976. When the film was released in the States, movie critics wrote glowingly of the movie and of Hopper's performance. They hoped he was fulfilling the promise he had shown in younger days and one went so far as to say that he "has perhaps never been better."

Unfortunately, while Dennis vindicated himself as an actor, few people saw the result. The movie failed to be a box office winner in the United States, and even with its Australian bush-ranger story, it did poorly in Australia as well.

Mad Dog Morgan was the first of three films of the 1970s in which Dennis showed his acting talent had ripened to fruition. They proved that the seeds of advice planted by Jimmy Dean and the Actors Studio training Dennis had grabbed for himself had taken root in fertile ground. The next stop in Hopper's travels would be the Philippines to appear in *Apocalypse Now*, the second of the films in which he would strut his stuff. Director Francis Ford Coppola wanted him there to play the part of Hurley, a spaced-out photojournalist covering the war in Southeast Asia.

Dennis arrived by helicopter at the location at Pagsanjan, in the Philippine backcountry far from Manila, in early September 1976. He came directly from Brussels, where he had just completed his part in a Belgian-French production called *Couleur Chaire*. He brought as his companion Caterine Milinaire, a photographer and writer. He was to spend six weeks in the Philippines, then fly directly to Hamburg, West Germany, for another film, without a stop to replenish himself at his refuge in Taos.

Apocalypse Now, which Coppola also wrote, was based partly on Joseph Conrad's "Heart of Darkness," set in the African Congo. Using the Conrad story as a starting point for inspiration, the movie was to be Coppola's masterful statement about the war in Vietnam, and about the horror of all wars. More than a treatise on war, however, the film would be the story of a manhunt that became one man's journey into himself, the tale of a soldier who believed he went in search of a lunatic only to find the madness within himself.

The stars of *Apocalypse Now* were Marlon Brando, playing the role of Colonel Kurtz, a renegade Green Beret carrying on his own private war in the jungle; and Martin Sheen as the Green Beret sent by his superiors up the river into Cambodia after Kurtz to terminate his command "with extreme prejudice." The photographer Hopper played is a follower of Kurtz, living in his compound, who greets Sheen when he arrives to assassinate the colonel.

Apocalypse Now represented a juicy part for Dennis, plus the chance to fulfill a couple of long-held aspirations. First, it allowed him to act out an ambition he had held during the war in Vietnam. He said, "I'd done everything I really wanted to do in photography except go to Vietnam, and I'd been turned down for that." So Coppola's film gave him a chance to live that out for a short time. It felt natural for him to be walking around with several camera straps around his neck again, talking to people from behind the protective mask of the lenses. However, it was not enough to inspire him to return to photography in earnest. Once he was out of that character it was on to the next one; he did not feel the need to play the Tourist in between.

The greater aspiration the part fulfilled was the opportunity finally to perform with Brando, an actor who had profoundly influenced Dennis Hopper when he was much younger. In recalling his early role models he said, "When I was a kid, it was Orson Welles and Barrymore. Then when I was thirteen, I saw Marlon Brando and Montgomery Clift in movies the same week, and it changed my life. My thinking about acting changed to trying to figure out what an internal actor was and what these people were doing."

Before *Apocalypse Now* was released, Hopper boasted, "It's going to be mind-shattering, because Brando and I go toe-to-toe for fifteen rounds, and you know what? I think I took the gorilla in Manila! I've never had a chance to go the distance with a great actor on an equal footing. But this time I did, and I think I got him."

That was the legend Hopper wanted to promote, but the facts of the matter came out later. In actuality, Brando would not allow Dennis to be on the set with him. Scenes in which they both appear were done so that they did not have to be on camera at the same time.

Dennis, in a less boastful mood several years later, explained how that worked: "I'd do my scenes while listening on tapes to what he did. He didn't want us to be on the set at the same time. I came on one night, and they said, 'This guy who used to be a baseball pitcher is going to throw bananas at you, because last night Brando called you a whimpering dog and threw bananas at you.' So all night this guy's throwing bananas at me. I thought, 'Weird, but that figures.' We never had a good relationship. Brando is more creative than most actors, and because of that maybe I was giving off something that freaks him out."

Bananas thrown at him was the least of the hardships Dennis had to face during filming. The location shooting in the rain forests of the Philippines was difficult. It was a heroic task to coordinate the logistics of transporting and maintaining a huge film crew under primitive conditions in rough terrain. Hopper was filled with admiration for Coppola the director. He empathized and remembered his own experiences in Peru directing *The Last Movie,* where he had similar difficulties but on a smaller scale—an $850,000 budget compared to the estimated $30 million *Apocalypse Now* would eventually cost. Dennis was lucky he had to stay for just a few weeks, unlike the crew and some of the cast, who had been suffering the intense heat and slogging through mud for months.

One of Hopper's scenes went through thirty-eight takes, from eight in the morning until six at night, before Coppola called it quits, and even then he was not completely satisfied. In the scene were extras playing severed heads who had to sit in boxes, buried up to their necks in mud. Dennis narrowly missed stepping right in the face of one of the female extras. Instead of smashing her face, he collapsed part of the container she sat in. Impressed with the willingness of these people to be subjected to such treatment, Dennis later said, "It seemed strange to me, but they didn't seem to mind. They got 'em out for lunch, too. Francis is a very patient man. So am I."

Dennis thought he and Coppola represented a dying breed of filmmakers. He compared this stage of big-budget moviemaking with gigantic crews to the cathedral builders of the Middle Ages.

He explained his theory to Eleanor Coppola, the director's wife, when she interviewed him for a documentary film she was shooting about the making of *Apocalypse Now.* She wrote in her diary, later published in a book called *Notes:*

> One of the things he said that interested me most was that he thought filmmaking was in the same phase of development that art was during the cathedral build-

ing period. When they built those great cathedrals in Europe, they employed stonemasons, engineers, fresco painters, etc., and they created the work through the combined talents of many. By the nineteenth century, art evolved to the point where the major work of the day was being done by individual artists working alone at an easel. Dennis was making the point that now filmmaking involves the talents of many departments and perhaps eventually major films will be made by one person with a video port-a-pack.

Whereas he had been the quintessential Australian bandit when he played Daniel Morgan, in *Apocalypse Now* he was playing a 100 percent American character, an idealistic naif who had gotten himself into a bad situation but was looking for the good in it, willing to believe that Kurtz was a divine genius. He eagerly tries to justify the severed heads and dead bodies hanging all around Kurtz's compound. He is seduced by the commander's insane intelligence and taken in by Kurtz's acting ability and artistic sensitivity as displayed in his poetry readings.

Hopper played Hurley as a hopped-up personality, desperate for his next fix, though it is never clear what he is hooked on. His hands fly up and down as he searches his burnt-out brain for words with which to express the wonders he has witnessed. He flinchingly grabs for a cigarette when the other Americans arrive at Kurtz's compound, but it is obvious that he did not achieve that level of craziness from ingesting tar and nicotine.

His relationship to Kurtz mirrors, somewhat, the relationship Hopper and Brando had on the set. On Hurley's side, he feels worshipful fear of the colonel. Kurtz, rather than appreciating the photographer's admiration for him, instead seems disgusted by him.

Dennis made a big impact in the part, considering how small and thematically incidental to the main plot his role was. By the end of the film, the photographer is insignificant to the story line. Coppola does not resolve what happens to him after Kurtz is killed. In the dramatic buildup to the final moments of the film, that character's fate becomes unimportant; he is just another one of the disillusioned in the multitude left behind in Kurtz's compound.

The reaction of many people who saw the film was that Dennis was just being himself. To a large degree he was. A member of Coppola's crew who went to the Philippines said, "The way he played Hurley was the way Dennis was acting off camera in those days. He was pretty messed up. There was no problem for anyone who wanted cocaine to get it there; it was shipped in with the equipment and supplies for the film. The government was so corrupt—they only cared about the money that this huge film production was bringing in—the crates were never searched, never went through customs.

"But with Dennis it wasn't just the drugs. He's got a tremendous energy that really comes across, a creative energy that's amazing."

His detractors discounted the naturalness of his performance as though it exhibited no talent for acting. But if Hopper's only ability was to portray himself, that did not explain how he went on to Hamburg to play a character entirely different and distinct from the freaked-out Hurley.

The night before he left the Philippines, Hopper and Coppola got drunk together at Coppola's house near the location site. They celebrated the completion of Dennis's part in *Apocalypse Now* and promised to work together again in the future. Panicked production people were trying to gather Dennis up to leave for Manila before the curfew, but Dennis would not go as long as there was beer left in the house. He had to be on a flight to Hamburg at six the next morning, and there was no way he would be able to get to the airport on time if he did not leave before the curfew fell. He was already three days late to his assignment in Germany, where he had a leading role.

Eleanor Coppola described the scene in her diary:

> Dennis was pretty drunk and in no mood to leave. Francis said, "Dennis, pick anyplace in the world, you'll be the star of a movie I'll make. The deal is, I promise I won't think about what the movie is going to be before we start. We'll just make it, we'll make it real fast, in three weeks, and it will be terrific. Pick a place." Dennis was saying, "Okay, okay, yeah." Francis and I waited to hear what exotic place it was going to be. Finally, Dennis said, "San Francisco." He said his wife (Daria Halprin) and child were there. . . . Francis said, "Okay, that's the story, that's where the story is. We'll do it." The production guy whose responsibility it was to get Dennis to Manila was getting pale. I asked Francis to help get Dennis going. Finally, after another half hour of noise and hugging and kissing and carrying on, Dennis and Caterine got into the car and on their way.

In early November 1976, Dennis was plunged from the steaming heat of the Philippine jungle into the bracing cold of autumnal northern Germany. There he joined an international cast of German, French, and American actors in *Der amerikanische Freund* (*The American Friend*). He was pleased at the prospect of being reunited with some old friends. Nicholas Ray, the director of *Rebel Without a Cause*, had a featured role in the film Dennis was about to star in. Also appearing in a smaller part was Sam Fuller, the American producer-director-screenwriter who had played the character of the director in Hopper's *The Last Movie*.

The American Friend was directed by German filmmaker Wim Wenders. Wenders was known for his difficult, idiosyncratic films, but this time he planned a different type of movie, a thriller with linear plot development. The story is of a basically good and innocent man, Hamburg picture framer Jonathan Zimmerman, who is driven to become a murderer by his own fear of death, abetted by the machinations of a French gangster. Hopper is a shady art dealer who is instrumental in putting Zimmerman and the gangster together, then befriends the picture framer. His character's name is Tom Ripley, and he is the American friend.

The opening scenes of the movie show Ripley picking up a painting from an artist, Derwatt (played by Nicholas Ray). Ripley and the artist have faked Derwatt's death in order to drive up the price of his paintings. Ripley is the art dealer who keeps discovering heretofore unknown Derwatt paintings. At the auction of the painting, Ripley meets the picture framer Zimmerman (played by Bruno Ganz) who, Ripley learns from the gallery owner, is dying of a rare blood disease. When Ripley mentions this to the French gangster Minot, the Frenchman sees an opportunity to use Zimmerman as a hit man to kill two other gangsters, one in France and one back in Germany.

Minot approaches Zimmerman with an offer of money, enough to give his family a good life after he dies. Minot tries to convince him that he has nothing to lose, since he is dying anyway. Zimmerman is at first disgusted by the idea of committing murder. Minot persists, and in addition to the money, offers to take Zimmerman to another doctor, a specialist in blood diseases, to see if there is any hope for him. Zimmerman begins to panic, believing his doctor has not told him everything about his disease. His doctor can give him only the vaguest of answers to questions about the progress of his illness; his prognosis is that Zimmerman may live for another two days, for one month, or for five years. Fearing he is close to death and wanting to provide for his wife and young son, Zimmerman agrees to go to Paris to see the specialist. In France, the doctor's report that Minot shows him offers no hope. Zimmerman performs the first hit in a

Paris Metro station but then decides he will not do the second one.

Meanwhile, Ripley has been coming to Zimmerman's shop and developing a friendship with him. He seems to feel guilty over the situation he has created by telling Minot about Zimmerman's condition. When he learns that Zimmerman is forced into killing again, the second time on a train from Munich to Hamburg, to the picture framer's complete surprise Ripley appears on the train to stop the murder but instead ends up helping with the assassination of two gangsters.

The conclusion of the film shows the damage Zimmerman's secret life and guilt over the murders do to his marriage. His wife leaves him just before the confederates of the murdered gangsters come after him and Ripley for revenge. They kill again to save themselves and take a wild ride to the sea to dispose of the bodies. Zimmerman leaves Ripley babbling drunkenly on the beach and then, as he is driving along the highway back home, he dies.

The American Friend rounded out the triptych of films that showcased the acting ability of Hopper during the 1970s. He transformed himself totally from the crazed photojournalist of *Apocalypse Now*, bopping around unshaven with a hippie headband holding back his long, flowing hair. Now he was Tom Ripley, a smoothly sinister underworld type with mysterious motivations for the suspicious activities he is involved in: Was he trying to get rid of Zimmerman because he might call attention to the strange after-"death" change in Derwatt's style (raising the possibility that Ripley's finds were forgeries), or was he just trying to help the terminally ill man?

As the American friend, Hopper plays a dangerous innocent. He is naive enough to claim innocence of knowing how Minot would use the information he gives him to trap Zimmerman into committing murder. Ripley just wants to be friends, he wants Zimmerman to like him. And he is willing to go as far as murder to earn that friendship. In the end he is hurt and surprised that Zimmerman abandons him on the beach, but Zimmerman has seen that Ripley is a danger to himself and to others.

There were a few elements of Hopper himself in the character he played: a man with a good eye for art who likes to wear cowboy hats and boots. The character of Ripley also shared Dennis's affection for the bottle.

Yet it was a performance. It was controlled acting, without the wild, distracting mannerisms critics complained about in his *Tracks* outing. It was clearly more than Dennis being himself while the cameras were rolling, as a few had judged some of his past screen appearances to be.

If anyone had doubts about Dennis Hopper as an actor, they needed only to look at these three films to be reassured that the man possessed talent. *Mad Dog Morgan*, *Apocalypse Now*, and *The American Friend* showed a diversity and range of ability that had only been hinted at in the early years of his career. Years later, after performances that were more highly praised in movies that were more widely seen, Dennis would still look back on *The American Friend* as one of his favorites. He told a reporter, *"The American Friend* is probably my best film, my most complete movie."

In the United States, *The American Friend* was seen only by a handful of critics and a small audience of Wim Wenders film buffs when it was released in 1977. In spite of Wenders's avowed attempt to make a straightforward thriller, it was not an easy movie to understand. It lacked the clear-cut plot development that would grab a mass audience. In spite of any disappointment he felt over the film's poor showing at the box office, Dennis had no regrets about working for Wim Wenders. He would later say that, from his point of view as an actor, Wenders was one of his favorite directors.

Dennis was maturing as an actor, but not as a person.

He was still the bad, rebellious boy, doing whatever society told him not to. He abused himself, drinking booze and taking drugs, and this led to further behavior the establishment found unbearable. He had violent outbursts; he liked to carry loaded guns. He couldn't be relied upon to behave as expected in polite society. Most directors did not want to deal with an actor who got drunk and smoked pot to prepare for his scenes.

An observer who worked on the production of *The American Friend* said, "At the time, it seemed that Wim was the only one who could control Dennis. He would listen to Wim and stay cool enough to get the work done." But that control lasted only as long as they were working on the movie. Wenders accompanied Hopper on a trip to Mexico that ended with Hopper being escorted to a plane and asked to leave the country. They had gone there thinking about making a movie in Mexico. While he was there, Dennis also presided over the first screening in that country of *Easy Rider*. Hopper said, "I am very happy that the problem with my film is over, as Mexico was one of the only countries in the world which vetoed its showing. . . . Now I feel like I'll be presiding over the film's world premiere."

Hopper became friendly with the wife of the Mexican president, who was involved in promoting her country's film industry. That connection proved lucky when he was reported to be in trouble for shooting guns in a Mexican town; instead of landing in jail, he was taken to the airport and asked to leave the country immediately.

Back in the United States, Dennis rested from his globetrotting, replenishing himself in the clean air and solitude of Taos. He put the big Luhan mansion up for sale, asking a quarter of a million dollars. It was just too big for him and only encouraged visitors to come and stay. Dennis claimed that he had only spent one night in it himself. He closed a deal for his asking price in January 1978 and moved the old

Spanish furniture he wanted to keep into the smaller house, where he had been living all along. It was advantageously situated on the Taos Indian reservation. That really came in handy after one of Hopper's drunken sprees in town.

"It's cool living on Indian land," Dennis said at the time, "because if you get juiced up in town and get into trouble, the local cops can't touch you. Dig this, man, the feds have to come out. They have to stand on this side of the little bridge that connects this house with the rest of the complex. And they're kind of embarrassed. 'Er, ah, Mr. Hopper, could you possibly come over here for just a moment?'"

Dennis still liked to laugh at authority and play the rebel. He also continued to seriously rail against the movie establishment for the way Universal Studios had treated *The Last Movie*. "That movie won the Venice Film Festival in 1971," he was constantly reminding people, "yet Universal never even distributed it outside this country. They gave me $1.1 million to shoot *Last Movie*. Hell, they can do that anytime they want. They write off $800,000 even if they only spend $150,000 on distribution and publicity. A year later they sell the outtakes back to their own company for $1 million for a TV show. So now they've made money without even distributing the movie! But they couldn't do that with *The Last Movie* without my permission because I had final cut."

In 1978 Hopper decided to exchange the outtakes from *The Last Movie* for the distribution rights. In the meantime, he took the film around to university campuses. "I've been doing the college lecture tour. I hit a few schools, show *The Last Movie*, then open the house to questions. Besides trying to get a feel about the film, I'm also interested in seeing what people feel in the universities these days. After all, we're not trying to stop a war anymore. I thought it would mean they could work harder and not be bothered. But I've found they're all a little bored—they want a cause to come along.

127

They ask me, 'What are we supposed to do? You're supposed to be our spokesman.'

"So I tell them, 'Look, don't you think I'm a little old to be your spokesman? I'm forty-two, for chrissakes. Why don't you just study and have a good time?' See, I have no bones to pick anymore, no chip on my shoulder. And it's not just because I'm older. Look, I think Jane Fonda and I won the war, but I'm not going to run for the fuckin' Senate. For me, it's over. And hell, I can't say that my politics hurt me in Hollywood. It was probably my own dogmatic personality."

It was that dogmatic, stubborn streak that would not let Dennis give up on *The Last Movie*. Once he got the distribution rights for the film, he announced plans to release it in Europe and in South America.

And he waited for the release of Coppola's film. Coppola was agonizing in an editing room in San Francisco over how to structure the movie. He was working in the shadow of his previous success and worried how *Apocalypse Now* would be received in comparison with his hugely popular *The Godfather*. The actors were all under contract not to discuss the film until its release, but Hopper felt he could reveal that "Francis said he could promise me at least a nomination," referring to the Academy Awards. Dennis was sure that *Apocalypse Now* would be "the greatest movie America has produced since *Gone With The Wind*." Once it came out, he figured, it was just a matter of time before the offers would be pouring in.

CHAPTER ELEVEN

The release of *Apocalypse Now* in 1979 did not herald a new age of constant work as Dennis would have liked; the scripts did not rain down on him. He settled back down in Taos to play with friends like Dean Stockwell, Russ Tamblyn, and musician Neil Young for a while. They even made a movie together. But Dennis had a restless energy that needed to be worked off, even if it meant not waiting for quality work. He never stopped working by choice. He was always willing to move on to the next job without a break, as when he had gone from the Philippines to Germany. Eventually his agent would convince him to move back to Los Angeles or face the prospect of remaining unemployed and forgotten in New Mexico. He took another stab at living in Tinseltown, but Dennis could not hack that phony scene for long and fled back to Taos.

And always he was headed ever downward on a spiral slick with alcohol and drugs. There would be moments when work was enough to temporarily straighten him out, but those times were fleeting and infrequent. There would be no turning upward until he had hit rock bottom.

The playtime in Taos was spent filming a movie called *Human Highway*, produced by Neil Young and credited to a whole raft of writers, including its director Bernard Shakey, co-producer Jeanne Fields, James Beshears, and actors Russ Tamblyn and Dean Stockwell. The stars were Young, Tamblyn, Stockwell, Hopper, Charlotte Stewart, Sally Kirkland, and Geraldine Baron. The New Wave musical group Devo also made an appearance.

There were months of hanging out together, while Young and others involved in the film scouted locations around Taos. Nights were spent trying to drink each other under the table in local bars. They would spend the evenings trading off performances: Dennis would recite a Shakespearean soliloquy if Neil would perform a few songs for the folks at the Sagebrush Inn.

The filming of the movie ended up in a shambles. Most of the cast and crew were stoned much of the time and their behavior was out of control.

Human Highway added to the violent, drug-freak legends surrounding Hopper. He and Neil Young were dragged into court by outraged co-star Sally Kirkland. She accused Dennis of having one of his violent outbursts during the filming and sued him, Young, and the production company for $2 million in damages over an incident between her and Dennis.

Kirkland alleged that Hopper had deliberately severed the tendon of her right index finger with a knife while under the influence of drugs. She blamed Young, as producer, for failing to keep his star under control. Her suit claimed that Dennis and others on the set were "smoking and in other ways ingesting dangerous and illegal drugs and drugs known to cause violence and dangerous behavior." She accused the producers of having "condoned said activity, believing it would increase the enthusiasm of those actors and others involved in the film, resulting in a better film and enhanced profits."

The alleged attack took place on the set where Dennis was fooling around with a knife, banging it on the furniture. This disturbed Kirkland, who tried to grab it from him. In the struggle, she claimed he deliberately cut her.

She said the wound required surgery that put her in the hospital for two days. No criminal charges were ever filed against Dennis, and a jury eventually found him innocent of the civil charges, but the reports in the press added to his wild-man reputation.

Dennis got more attention from the real-life courtroom drama he starred in than *Human Highway* got in the theaters. The biggest audience the film had was probably the jury who had to watch it at Hopper's trial, even though the cameras were not running when the alleged attack took place.

Before Kirkland filed her suit, Hopper was already on his way to Canada. He still had friends who were loyal to him and steered work his way when they could; he had done the same for them when he was in a position to. In early 1980, Paul Lewis, who had worked as producer on *Easy Rider* and on *The Last Movie*, was executive producer on a Canadian project intended as a made-for-television movie. He brought Dennis in to play the role of an alcoholic father, opposite Sharon Farrell as his wife and Linda Manz as the juvenile delinquent daughter. "I saw no redeeming qualities in the father whatsoever," Dennis later revealed, but he did not want to let Lewis down so he took the part against the advice of his managers.

The original screenplay for a movie to be called "The

Case of Cindy Barnes" was written by Leonard Yakir and Brenda Nielson. Yakir was also making his debut as director of the film. Two weeks into filming, executive producer Lewis was in a panic—they had only two and a half hours of film, none of which he considered worthwhile, and Hopper had not even been before the cameras yet.

Dennis later recalled, "I was there two weeks and never worked. And Paul Lewis said, 'Hey, you gotta come see the rushes, there's nothing usable!' And I said, 'Nobody said you were a critic of artists, right? The guy's never directed a film, let him alone.'"

But there was no improvement and Lewis was ready to abandon the project. "Friday night in the toilet Paul tells me, 'I'm leaving the picture, but your money's in escrow. Everything's cool for you.'" Dennis, however, was interested in doing the film, not just getting his money. "By that time I'd met Linda Manz, and I'd known Sharon Farrell before, and I'd been getting my wardrobe together—I was ready to play the father. So I said, 'Hey, wait a second. Let me see what you got.'"

Paul told him how little was on film at the end of two weeks. Dennis still wanted to see. "On Saturday I went and looked at the two and a half hours. There was no usable footage at all."

But where Lewis saw disaster, Hopper saw opportunity, if he could just convince the financial backers to let him take over the director's chair. Over the weekend he and Lewis met with the money men. They agreed to give him free rein in directing the movie, and with Dennis as director, his friend Paul agreed to stay on as producer. The only issue the backers wouldn't budge on was that he would have to use Canadian-born Raymond Burr, of the *Perry Mason* television series fame, so that the film would still qualify as a Canadian tax shelter.

Dennis did not have much use for Burr, since he had

already decided to change the whole concept of the film. But he reluctantly agreed to the requirement; he was desperate to direct another film. He could not believe this chance had fallen into his lap when he least expected it. He would find a way around the restrictions—he certainly would not have Burr do the corny voice-over narration called for in the original script. Dennis proudly proclaimed, "I do not do movies with narration!" He was probably more anxious to do well with the film than the financers were: Dennis hoped it would put him back on the map where Hollywood could find him.

Shooting with Hopper as director began at six o'clock Monday morning. He had spent Sunday beginning the rewrite and recasting all but the central figures in the story. Rewriting went on as the movie was being shot, and made for a film quite different from the one Dennis had initially signed to do. He described his input to the final product: "There was no punk involvement in the original, and the daughter didn't play drums or guitar. Her mother wasn't a junkie, and it was all narrated by Raymond Burr. Originally he was the hero of the film. It was, like, the case history of Cindy Barnes and how Raymond Burr saved her as a child psychologist."

In the movie Dennis made, no one was saved in the end. As Dennis told one reporter, "All my pictures end in fire." The film focuses on a young girl, CeBe, who idolizes her father who has been in prison for manslaughter. He went behind bars for five years for ramming his truck into a stalled school bus, killing many of the children on board, when he was drunk. While he is put away, CeBe creates idealistic fantasies about him and her other hero, Elvis Presley. Her mother is a drug addict who has become the mistress of the man who owns the restaurant where she waits tables.

When her father is released from prison, CeBe's hopes for a brighter future are dashed to bits. He is soon fired from his job driving a tractor in a garbage dump. He finds out who was responsible for his firing: the father of a kid who was killed on the school bus he plowed into. Backed up by a violent buddy, Hopper robs the man and arrives back home with his friend, both of them drunk. He then tries to push his friend into having sex with CeBe. This episode rekindles CeBe's memories of her father molesting her as a child. She kills Hopper, then gets into the cab of the wrecked truck that sits in their backyard. She commits suicide, taking her mother with her when she blows the wreckage up.

All the changes left little for Raymond Burr to do. Dennis remembered, "By the time Burr got there to do his part, I'd changed the whole concept. And he didn't know this. He got there, ready to do his thing. And the investors insisted on Burr, because they had to qualify for the Canadian tax shelter.

"He didn't like the script, not knowing that I had thrown it away and that he was only going to be in two scenes. I said, "Well, rewrite it—rewrite it any way you want." And so in three days, for the $50,000 he got, I did a whole television show. I shot everything he rewrote, knowing I was only going to use two scenes." He filmed about fifteen scenes with Burr, including an entirely different ending. Thirteen of those scenes wound up on the cutting room floor.

Dennis was back in his element, behind the camera. He shot quickly, completing the shooting schedule in four weeks and two days. He expressed his directing philosophy as: "Keep moving! When in doubt, give 'em a setup. 'Put the camera here! Light it!'"

"I try to figure out a way to utilize as much of my set as possible," he further expounded. "And without losing story content. Setting the camera so they're moving. Moving the actors through it, so they know where they're going. See what plays. And, in this instance, I would go through and do the whole thing myself, by myself. Set the camera. And then, while they were lighting, take the actors through their paces, work with the actors between shots. The most important thing is just to keep the next shot coming. Make sure that your crew isn't dragging ass. Make sure you got a shot going next. As soon as that shot's finished, you got another setup, so your actors are working constantly, so that they're not all sitting in dressing rooms screwing around. It's really important to keep them moving. And also keep your crew moving. Keep them busy all the time."

As for his relationship to the other actors, he said, "It's funny, in four weeks and two days a lot comes back. Line readings. Screaming and yelling. Back to all those devices I really fought against as an actor. What most directors don't know about is acting. I know a little bit about it. There aren't really too many directors who like actors. And I get the feeling now that it's becoming more mechanical, with all the new computers and devices, videos and so on. They don't even trust themselves. They have to look at the video five or six times. I'm just from a little different school—not UCLA, but the factory floor!"

Working with an editor on one Movieola, the film was ready in six weeks, a record in speedy editing for Dennis. For the sound track, he decided to use a song written and performed by his friend Neil Young, "Out of the Blue," which also gave the film its title. That same year, 1980, *Out of the Blue* premiered at the Cannes Film Festival, where it was well received. Canada did not want it presented as a Canadian feature at the festival; it was introduced simply as "a Dennis Hopper film." Dennis joked that "It was the first entry from Mars."

The movie was a hit in England and France, but it took nearly two years to make its way to an opening in the United States. When it did, Dennis willingly hit as many talk shows and other interview forums as would have him on to promote the film, so it might be seen by the audience it was meant for, the people that it was really about. He said, "In many ways it's maybe my best film. People who hate it have a real problem. It's about the society of North America; the family unit is falling apart. People who say all this doesn't exist in this country—where have they been?"

He went on to explain, "You could say the father and mother probably saw *Easy Rider*, and that the father was probably a biker in his day. I wanted to show a girl wanting to be a boy, emulating her father but still wanting to put on lipstick and be a little ballerina. But I can't make any moral judgments about the positive and negative aspects of the story. I feel it's like a time capsule film—it's like a little article on the fourth page of a newspaper that says that a kid's killed her mother and father, and you wonder what that's about and then move along."

At the urging of his manager, Dennis moved back to Los Angeles when he completed *Out of the Blue*. It was time for him to be seen around town again, to show people that he was still alive and kicking, ready for work. But he wasn't prepared to play the game the way everyone else did. He said, "I came back to remind people that I'm still around," but he also said, "I'm not going to any Hollywood parties. I'm not going to eat at those restaurants where actors go to be seen." Even after coming back, he still worked in Europe as much as in Hollywood: He appeared in a Spanish film called *Reborn* and in *White Star*, a German film.

At home he was offered parts to play that were supporting roles to unknown hopefuls who were expected to be the next hot thing on the scene. He appeared in a Casablanca–Polygram Pictures film called *King of the Mountain*. It co-starred two handsome newcomers, Harry Hamlin and Joseph Bottoms. The story was about illegal drag racing along Mulholland Drive, a famous winding road through posh neighborhoods at the top of the Hollywood Hills. As the film opens, Steve (Harry Hamlin) is the current "king of the mountain," the best and fastest of the bunch, and he wants to hold on to his title. His roommate, Buddy (Joseph Bottoms), is also a racer, but is really more interested in his career as an aspiring composer-musician-performer. They have a third roommate named Roger (Richard Cox), who doesn't care about cars; his only interest is being a successful record producer.

Hopper's role was as Cal, a has-been "king of the mountain," past his prime. He appeared in the film looking very burnt-out, generally rumpled and unkempt. He was given some awful lines of dialogue; for instance, referring to Hamlin's character, Cal says, "He's drunk with the speed of his youth."

Perhaps mercifully there wasn't much of Dennis's performance to see because so much of the film was devoted to the racing. However, most of these scenes were filmed at night and therefore were not as exciting as they might have been. The cars were difficult to see, so that what could have been the highlights of the picture were mostly just headlights zipping by.

All of the characters in *King of the Mountain* were non-stop drinkers—mostly consuming beer, but also great quantities of white wine, Scotch, and Jack Daniels. However, no one but Hopper's Cal ever appeared to get drunk. This was just one in a series of drunken characters Hopper would essay over the next few years.

There were no directing jobs offered, nor any he could pick up accidentally as he had with *Out of the Blue*. But there was some continuing demand for his acting talents. Coppola used him again, but not to do the film they had drunkenly pledged in the Philippines to make together in San Francisco. The location was Oklahoma and Dennis was to play another alcoholic father, in *Rumble Fish*. Once again he was a supporting player to a couple of promising, but at the time relatively unknown young actors, Matt Dillon and Mickey Rourke, who played his alienated sons in the film.

Dennis saw that he was entering a new phase of his career. He said, "I realized that I'm at a transitional age. I need to work through it as an actor, from being the son to being the father, from being the patient to being the doctor. There are periods in an actor's life: In your twenties you have to play teenagers. If you get through that, in your thirties you get to play adults. Then in your forties there's this transition I have to go through now.

"Especially if you were never a star. A star has maybe three years of being a star, then you never hear about them. There are thousands of guys like that—three years, that's about your basic star period. I didn't really go in for that."

It had to hurt, though, that he had never been one of those stars. Of the actors he had admired, like Brando or Barrymore or Welles, each one had at least had his moment in the spotlight, a time, however brief, of leading-man roles. Dennis had missed that career phase, and however much he protested at this point that he had never pursued it, it was just that call to stardom that had first lured him to Hollywood.

Dennis was going through another transition that had nothing to do with acting. He was moving toward a reconciliation with his father, who was gravely ill. He feared that Jay Hopper did not have much longer to live and he wanted to do something to please him, make a gesture that would in a small way begin to heal some of the hurt feelings between them. After his father's death, Dennis told a reporter, "I drank quite excessively, like a lot, and for years, but my father was dying and I wanted him to see me sober for the last year of his life."

Dennis was nibbling around the edges of sobriety, but he had not embraced it as a total way of life. He still felt it was sometimes necessary for him to use alcohol in his work. He was supposed to be abstaining when he played the part of the alcoholic father in Coppola's film but, as he said at around that time, "There are some scenes where you should be drunk, not act drunk." The scene in *Rumble Fish* was set in a bar where he drunkenly confronts his son, Rusty James, played by Matt Dillon. "I told Francis, 'If we don't get it after the third take, I'm going to start taking shots of cognac.' Francis said no, no, he didn't want me to go back to drinking, but I told him it would be okay. We shot for eighteen hours, I consumed a bottle of cognac, and I stopped drinking again the next day."

But his hold on abstinence was tenuous. Dennis was not as free of his addiction to alcohol as he wanted to believe. There were reports that he was drinking beer and smoking grass in his dressing room to prepare himself for scenes in *The Osterman Weekend*, another film he appeared in during his Hollywood sojourn. He amazed his fellow actors on the film by being able to work once he arrived on the set from his dressing room.

Dennis later explained, "My problem wasn't working. My problem was personal. My problem was getting out of the dressing room to the set. Not getting out of the dressing room to the set on time, but the emotional problems I had just to make the walk. You know, you're doing drugs in the dressing room, and spooking everybody on the set and so on, and that's the reputation that should be really talked about, not the work, because I got to the set on time. I did the work on time, I did good work. My personal life was a mess, a nightmare."

The Osterman Weekend was to be director Sam Peckinpah's comeback film, his first in five years, after battling heart ailments, career setbacks, and his own struggle with the bottle. The motion picture turned out to be a well-done film rendering of a convoluted story based on a Robert Ludlum novel. The tale shows a successful television journalist, played by Dutch actor Rutger Hauer, who is manipulated by a CIA chief with Presidential ambitions into believing that his best friends are actually Soviet agents. Hopper played the part of one of the friends, Richard Tremayne, a doctor whose wife is a cocaine addict. He is killed, along with the rest of the journalist's weekend guests, before the end of the movie. Sadly for Dennis, it was not an outstanding part, nor was the movie one that did particularly well upon its release in the fall of 1983.

Dennis finished work on *The Osterman Weekend* at the end of 1982. Complaining that it was costing him ten times more to live in his leased house in Los Angeles than it did to live in Taos, Dennis decided it was time to head for the hills again. He had kept his place in New Mexico when he reluctantly returned to California, and now he was glad he had a home to go back to.

But what had once been his sanctuary no longer seemed like such a safe place to Dennis. His girlfriend of the time, Elen Archuletta, could point to bullet holes in the walls of the house they shared. Dennis had put those there, shooting at imagined intruders and phantoms that only he could see. People who visited him left with tales of Hopper sleeping with a gun underneath his pillow and challenging people who approached the house to identify themselves or face the barrel of a gun.

People who were around Taos at that time said Dennis was frequently shooting guns, inside and outside the house. He complained of being persecuted by people. He said he saw ghosts. And he kept drinking; friends were afraid he would do himself injury with either the booze, the firearms, or with a lethal combination of the two.

They were worried about his sanity. He rediscovered a stunt called The Russian Suicide Death Chair that he was anxious to try. When he was promoting *Out of the Blue* in

Portland, Oregon, he invited everyone at a reception after the screening to come to the local speedway to watch him fold himself up under a chair wired with six sticks of dynamite. The plan was that when the dynamite was set off, the chair would disintegrate, but he would be safe inside the vacuum that would be created by the surrounding explosives, as though in the eye of a hurricane.

He had seen this stunt performed when he was a child. The Russian Suicide Death Chair was so named because it was supposed to have been used by the Bolsheviks during the Russian Revolution to fake the executions of certain nobility they actually wanted to save. If some of the sticks of dynamite failed to explode, however, the trick could be fatal.

The dynamite was ignited, and in a burst of fire the chair was blown apart. Out of a cloud of smoke and dust, Dennis emerged from the debris, unhurt but shaken. He gratefully hugged his stunt advisor and then turned to acknowledge the cheers of the crowd. When he chose to perform the stunt again during a retrospective of his work at Rice University in Texas, friends began to believe Dennis was more seriously deranged than they had ever imagined.

Dennis later said, "I thought it was worth risking because there was a contract out on me anyway." Trapped in a vicious circle composed of alcoholism and his cocaine habit, his paranoia grew by leaps and bounds as he spiraled ever downward. On a daily basis he was drinking a half gallon of rum, plus a few beers, balanced out by several grams of cocaine. The cocaine kept him up, so he wasn't stumbling around or passing out, and when the coke made him too jittery and uptight, a few drinks would calm him down again.

Dennis told BBC correspondent Barbra Paskin, "I would look at other people falling down and slurring words and I would say, 'I don't know what's wrong with these people. Why can't they handle their drinks?'" He was reported to say later, "I thought people who were falling down had problems. Not people who were standing up, drinking all the time—and then doing coke to keep drinking more. I also thought being an actor you had a license to drink."

His paranoia grew to the point where he believed that someone had put a contract out on his life, and suddenly not even his sanctuary in Taos seemed safe anymore. Once again, Hopper called on some friends to form an armed guard for him, this time to escort him to the airport in Albuquerque. He was going to get away from Taos before he was trapped there by whoever was out to complete that contract on him.

He flew to Los Angeles and checked into a hotel. From there he organized an apocalyptic orgy, a sort of condemned man's last request party. He said in a later interview, "I saw some people in Los Angeles and proceeded to have an orgy with some women that I knew." The cocaine had him so physically and emotionally numbed, he needed the maximum amount of stimulation he could get; if one woman wasn't enough, he'd bring in as many as it took to fulfill his sexual fantasy.

The drug itself had lost its punch, too. "At that point I started shooting cocaine," he later reported. The injections gave him that good old rush again, more than the first time he had snorted, so many years ago. The direct entry into the bloodstream gave him a nearly orgasmic effect, a heart-stopping tingling from head to toe. His whole body vibrated, in tune with the universe; he felt like God—for a few minutes. The high got into him faster, but it left more quickly as well. That overwhelming euphoria lasted only two or three minutes, and the afterglow was completely gone in the next ten or so.

"I shut myself up in a hotel for like three days," Dennis continued, "went through vast quantities of cocaine, shooting it every ten minutes, and vast quantities of women." He told another reporter, "I was shooting, like, cocaine and heroin together, just like Belushi." (John Belushi had died—overdosed on speedballs, the combined injection of heroin and cocaine—in a Los Angeles hotel room just months before Hopper's orgy.) "And I was moving from one town to another so fast. And I knew the Mafia was after me."

After the three-day, round-the-clock orgy in L.A., Dennis got on a plane to Houston, Texas. He went to confront a man he said was one of the heads of the Mafia in Texas, to find out about the contract on his life. They met in a deserted parking lot, where Hopper began questioning him about the hit. "I assumed he wasn't answering correctly, I pulled a knife on him."

For anyone else, this would have meant certain death. But the mafioso didn't touch him. The crime boss must have felt compassion for the insane creature before him and told his people not to hurt him.

Dennis was very close to the bottom, but he hadn't quite touched it yet. But when he crashed into the dead end, there would be no doubt he had arrived.

CHAPTER TWELVE

Inevitably, the years of excess and abuse had to take their toll on Dennis. It is hard to understand why his liver or kidneys did not give out, considering what his normal routine was for many years. As he later told BBC correspondent Barbra Paskin, "People would say, 'What about your drugs, your drug use?' I said, 'Hey, my drug use is really a cover, because I'm really an alcoholic.' And everybody'd go 'Ha, ha, ha.' And in point of fact, I was an alcoholic, and an open one, too. I was not a closet drinker. I drank all day long.

"I'd drink beer all day. At lunch I'd have a couple of martinis or whatever and I'd go back to beer. Then in the evening I would just start drinking whatever, Scotch and soda, or whatever, all night. And get up and work and do my thing. And this went on for years."

His body held up under the excesses and abuses heaped upon it. It was his brain that finally went under in the flood of booze and drugs. He was trying to make it to another job when his mind snapped.

Dennis had himself barely together enough to make it to Cuernavaca, Mexico, where he had a part in a movie called *Jungle Fever*. Ironically, he was hired to play the role of the head of the U.S. Drug Enforcement Agency in Mexico. He was still suffering from paranoid delusions, waiting for the hit man to get him.

Dennis arrived drunk and coked up. For a time he wanted to blame the episode that followed on LSD-spiked shots of tequila waiting for him in his hotel room. But the fact was that he had finally reached the end of his rope with alcohol and cocaine. A psychiatrist would diagnose him as paranoid schizophrenic, but Dennis thought he was still totally in control—the cocaine told him that. He believed everything he was seeing, hearing, and feeling was real.

After he checked into his hotel room, he later recalled, "I became convinced that there were people in the bowels of this place who were being tortured, and being cremated. That people had come to save me and they were being killed and tortured and it was my fault."

The hallucinations became stronger, and he felt trapped in the hotel. He could not stand being inside any longer. He walked out into the warm Mexican night, out of the town. He removed all his clothes—he said he could feel things crawling on him, snakes attacking him and bugs underneath his skin, coming out and creeping all over his body. Naked, he entered the jungle. He spent the whole night wandering through what he thought was a war zone. He later reported hearing voices and seeing visions, like alien spacecraft—mysterious lights that receded into the distance. He followed the glowing objects. He said he thought he had become his own solar system.

As the sun came up, Dennis, still naked, walked back into Cuernavaca. The police who came after him seemed to be part of the enemy forces in the war he was imagining. They tackled Dennis and tried to put a robe on him. He said, "When the police tried to get me dressed, I refused. I said, 'No, kill me like this!' I wanted to die naked."

The police finally wrestled him into a robe and took him to the small local jail. Dennis's hallucinations continued: "I heard friends of mine being lined up outside and machine gunned." Not wanting an overdosed American movie star dying in their jail, the police transferred him to a hospital. Horrified, Dennis watched the doctor approach him with a needle. Dennis remembered thinking, "I wouldn't take any injections because I thought they were going to kill me and then I thought my lungs had been replaced with these— other things."

Meanwhile, the film production manager had tracked him down. Some of the film crew went to the hospital to bring him back. When they saw him, they knew there was no way he would be able to stay in Mexico and work on *Jungle Fever*. In fact, they were anxious to get him away from the set before his activities brought the scrutiny of the law on all of them.

Two hulking stuntmen took Dennis to the Mexico City airport to accompany him on a Mexicana Airlines flight back to the States. Dennis imagined cameras everywhere, filming his every action; his life had become a movie. While the plane was waiting on the runway in Mexico City, Dennis looked out the window and thought he saw the wing burst into flames. That was the signal for him to make his getaway. He broke away from his guardians and tried to open an escape hatch and walk out onto the wing. Airline employees insisted that his companions would have to hold Hopper down and guarantee he would not get out of his seat again until the plane reached Los Angeles.

Back in L.A., friends checked him into Studio 12, a drug and alcohol rehabilitation facility geared especially toward movie industry people. He was still hearing voices. He later said the telephone wires were talking to him, giving him secret messages.

Soon after his arrival Dennis had a violent flare-up during which he grabbed a pair of hedge clippers and clipped away at everything in his path. He had to keep clipping; it was the only thing that made the maddening inner voices shut up. They wouldn't leave him alone unless he kept cutting, clipping, tearing into the hedges and bushes. When white-coated orderlies came to fit him for a straitjacket, they refused to understand about the voices. They just strapped him in so he couldn't clip anymore. The doctors started him on a regimen of antipsychotic drugs to cool down the violent eruptions.

Once he had calmed down, Dennis began to respond to the Studio 12 program, which relies in part on the Twelve Steps advocated by Alcoholics Anonymous for recovery from alcohol addiction. But he began suffering strange side effects from Prolixin, one of the antipsychotic drugs the doctors prescribed for him. He turned out to be one of a small percentage of patients who react badly to that medication.

For three months he was shaking as though he were afflicted with Parkinson's disease. He felt frozen, unable to move. He could not think clearly enough to form coherent sentences. He had trouble feeding himself; he could not manipulate a fork well enough to get the food to his mouth. He was nearly deprived of the one addiction he could indulge in while in the clinic: cigarettes. He shook so badly he could barely get one into his mouth to light it. His greatest fear was that he would never act again, given the shape he was in. If he could not work, life held no more interest for him.

He checked himself out of Studio 12 and Elen Archuletta, his girlfriend from Taos, drove his car out from New Mexico to pick him up and take him back home. Dennis recalled, "We're driving back to Taos and on the way there I told her that I was going to kill myself because I obviously wouldn't be able to act again. I couldn't even pick up a cigarette." She took him to a doctor, who knew enough to give him another drug, Cogentin, to counteract the Prolixin's side effects. The thrill he felt, just to be able to reach into his pocket for a Marlboro again, put it in his mouth, and light it—it was like he had come back from the dead.

With his return from the abyss, he thought it time to turn over a new leaf. He decided it was the booze that had been his downfall. He determined to stick with the Alcoholics Anonymous program and stay off liquor.

Speaking to Barbra Paskin he said, "I went into an alcohol-drug rehabilitation place, and when I came out of it, I decided, 'Well, right. Alcohol drove me insane. It's obvious: It was alcohol and it wasn't drugs.' So I wasn't drinking—because my whole life had been to have the martini before the meal, have the beer, have a beer with the meal, have an Irish coffee, cognac afterwards, and then drink the rest of the night. My whole orientation had been: 'Where's the drink, where's the drink, where's the beer?'

"So to get through that I decided I would just continue doing drugs, so that rather than having a beer in the morning, I would have cocaine. And I'd always thought, 'Well, I can stop cocaine anytime I want. It's not an addictive thing.'

"The point is not that cocaine is addictive or that beer is addictive; I'm an addictive personality.

"So I just started using cocaine like I was drinking beer all day. Suddenly, I became a secret person about it because now I was going to be straight." He continued his involvement with the A.A. program and really was staying off alcohol, but he could not let anyone know that he was still a drug addict.

In fact he was practicing incredible feats of self-denial by not facing up to his cocaine addiction. He had merely moved coke up to the primary spot alcohol had occupied for so long in his life. Now he was going through half an ounce of the white powder every two or three days—a heavy habit. It would have broken most people financially, forced them into dealing to support their habit. But Hopper had connections that most addicts did not.

"So I wouldn't let people know that I was doing cocaine. I had a half an ounce of cocaine in my pocket at all times. I was doing a half an ounce every two days, two and a half days, three days at the most. I was getting dealer's price—fifteen dollars a gram—when everybody was paying a hundred and fifty. There are a lot of dealers and people that were never my friends but that I dealt with because I had to."

He had to because he was hooked; he still felt that emptiness inside that he had been trying to fill with alcohol. Now he was pouring cocaine into it as fast as he could, ignoring the fact that this "snow" melted quickly and left the hole just as empty as ever.

He spent much of the remainder of 1983 and early 1984 in Taos. He had one film job during this time, under the direction of Robert Altman in a movie called *O.C. and Stiggs*. It was described as a "comedy in which two teenagers terrorize suburban America in a series of madcap escapades." Hopper's adult co-stars were Martin Mull and Jane Curtin. This film was shelved and was never seen in theatrical release, though it did finally surface on cable television in 1988. He had other work already in the can: During this time *Rumble Fish* and *The Osterman Weekend* were both released. Most of the time he spent bored, watching television, struggling with his personal demons.

"I did a year like that, without drinking. And then went totally crazy with it." He started hallucinating again. This time he could not blame it on the alcohol. He recalled the second trip to the bottom: "Again I was hearing voices. People came to see me. After they left I'd hear them being tortured and murdered. It's really amazing when the telephone wires start talking to you.

"I was going back to celebrate my first birthday in A.A. and decided that I was a drug addict also," he said a few years later when he was fully recovered. In April 1984 Dennis returned to Los Angeles and checked himself into Century City Hospital's drug and alcohol rehabilitation program. The hallucinations were strong and he was considered likely to do violence to himself or someone else. The doctors put him on antipsychotics again and transferred him to the psychiatric ward at Cedars-Sinai Hospital.

As his friend Jack Nicholson said, "Dennis tapped the bottom. He was staying at places that didn't allow visitors. It wasn't Sunnybrook Farm; no sashay through those rich men's rest homes. He did the real stuff."

For a while, things looked hopeless for Dennis. The state of California did not consider him to be responsible for his life. Although he had originally checked himself into the hospital, he would not be able to get out on his own. He walked around like a zombie, zoned out on Thorazine and other drugs to keep him passive. He had no family who would take responsibility: His daughters were too young, his father was dead, his mother had remarried and was distant from him, and all his wives were ex.

To the rescue came a friend from the old days, Bert Schneider. Schneider had been involved with the production of *Easy Rider* and had remained a loyal friend through all of Hopper's changes. He was incredulous that his friend was actually incarcerated and being further drugged into submission. He signed Dennis out and took him to his home to get him on the road to recovery.

Although Dennis balked at the idea of leaving the house on his own, Schneider insisted that he take responsibility for himself from the start. Over the actor's protestations, Schneider forced him to drive himself to appointments with a psychiatrist. Hopper also found some of his other friends who had already made dramatic changes in their lives were there for him, encouraging him to go straight.

Producer-screenwriter Randy Pike recalled, "I saw Dennis when he was drying out. Dean Stockwell was with him; he had a big input in his drying out. Stockwell was giving him moral support. When I saw him, he still looked a mess. He was burned out. He'd talk and he'd laugh at himself. He was overemotional and overreacted to situations."

It was a slow process to clear his mind again, but Dennis made steady progress, living life one day at a time. He threw away the antipsychotic drugs and renewed his involvement with Alcoholics Anonymous. This time he was ready to admit that his problem was with drugs as well as alcohol. He realized, in his words, "You've got to have a higher power. You can't get yourself sober, and no other human being can get you sober. The only thing that can get you straight is a higher power, a belief in a higher power than yourself."

His search for higher spirituality through chemicals had failed: He had not found God on an LSD trip. But, he said, "God found me. I was planning to leave myself out in the desert somewhere dead, and God said, 'Come on in. Why don't you come back and see some of your friends. They're dead too.'"

Dennis had decided he wanted to live. As he said later, "You either die or you change. Something in me wanted to live and I believe that 'something' was the part that must create."

In order to recover, so he could go on and create again, Dennis had to admit to himself that he was powerless in the face of his addictions. That had been the most difficult admission to make as long as he was under the influence of cocaine, because that drug, even when he was in the grip of his worst hallucinations, gave him the feeling that he was still in control, that he was the master of his fate. He had to come to the realization that his life was out of control, and that drugs had made it that way.

Once he accepted that he could not get himself straight alone, Dennis was ready to turn to the help he would need to get sober and stay sober. He experienced a spiritual rebirth that enabled him to accept the aid of—as he called it—the "higher power," what others might call God. He turned his problem over to the higher power and asked for help to find the solution.

Now that his head had begun to clear, Dennis had to face up to his past before he could get on with his future. He could not indulge in any more dangerous self-denial; that would be fatal to his recovery. He had to level with himself about his past behavior. It was also time for him to consider all the people he had hurt in the past, and to begin trying to make amends.

He cataloged each broken relationship, every violent outburst, each run-in he had had with authority figures, whether they were directors and producers or the police. Now he was able to connect all these heartbreaking times with alcohol and drugs. There was not one embarrassing moment or terrible fight he could remember having had when he was sober. Almost every bad situation he had experienced in his life had been fueled by his intake of booze and dope.

He had used chemicals to boost his confidence. He had done it from childhood, and as he got older and met more people who were also good at the same things he did, his confidence needed more propping up. He had lived almost his whole life comparing himself to a dead man, haunted by the thought that if Jimmy had lived, he would always have been better than Dennis, at everything: a better actor, a better director, a better photographer, a better painter.

He got drunk and stoned so he wouldn't have to feel so much, either. He ran from the guilt he felt when he lived and went on to prosper while Dean had been cut down before he could fulfill his destiny. He hid from his feelings of inadequacy for having let his parents down, knowing that he was not the son his mother had expected him to be. That successful doctor or lawyer dream was one he never shared with her. He had even tried to escape the anger he had for his folks' trying to push him to be what they wanted, and not what he knew he could be.

Finally, what he had to realize beyond any doubt was that no matter why he thought he drank and used drugs, the reasons didn't matter. What mattered was for him to understand that he could never take a drink or drugs again. If he took one drink, he would drink a half-gallon; one snort of cocaine would mean a half an ounce up his nose or into his veins.

His soul-searching led Dennis to emotional reconciliations with his mother and with his daughters. For many years he had selfishly believed he was only hurting himself by drinking and taking drugs. Now, his head clear of the cloud of booze and drugs, he could see how much he had harmed his family as well. None of his relationships stood a prayer as long as he was living in a perpetual state of inebriation, his personality distorted by liquor and chemicals. Having let down some of the defensive barriers of intoxication, he could allow others to get close to him for a change.

The introspection and recognition of his shortcomings, along with the willingness to right whatever wrongs he committed, had to become a lifelong habit for Dennis, to replace the harmful habits of using drugs and drink to escape from his own feelings and fill the emptiness in his life.

The final step in his recovery took place when he was ready to work with other alcoholics and addicts. He had to be firm in his own beliefs and be able to show that the principles he lived by were working for him. If A.A.'s Twelve Steps had saved him from the hell he had been living in, they could work the same miracle for others.

He told a reporter, "I work with people who want to get straight. It has nothing to do with kids; I don't work with people who are going to start out and do whatever they're going to do. I work with people who've bottomed out and want a new life. I don't think people can stop until they've bottomed out, spiritually and morally, or they die. That's how they get off drugs."

Dennis's newfound sobriety did not infuse him with a missionary zeal to reform everyone he knew. Many of the people he counted among his close friends were still heavily into alcohol and drugs. He said, "Now I find it extremely stupid and silly that people go running off with their little straw and their little bag and all the girls come with them."

He continued, "The ones that were my friends are still my friends. I've been through it all and they're still my friends. It's better for me to be straight. And eventually they're going to have to stop or die. I'm not out to stop anyone from using drugs. How can I try to reeducate them? They have to get to that point by themselves. I can't convince them till they're ready."

As for himself, he said, "It's great being sober. I don't have to go through the mood swings and the paranoia and the schizophrenia of using and wanting drugs and all the bullshit that goes with it. I've never been happier in my life."

CHAPTER THIRTEEN

Feeling more content than he had since his childhood walks into town to the movies with Grandma Davis, Dennis faced life head-on, ready to make up for all the time lost to drugs and alcohol. He held tightly to his Big Blue Book from Alcoholics Anonymous; it helped keep him on the straight and narrow path. Over the next three years he went about proving himself all over again. But this time he was not out to prove what an artistic genius he could be. That had to be something he knew within himself. The only way he could show it was through work, but to work he first had to demonstrate to directors and producers that they could rely on him to be there, on time, sober and ready to perform.

He was scared to death at first. Could he act without the help of his old friends, liquor and cocaine? He said, "The scariest time was when I finally got sober and I wondered if I'd be able to work again." But he had to find out. Now that he wasn't depleting himself on debauchery, he had energy to burn and needed to channel it into something positive.

He started out in a fairly low-key role, the part of a high-school science teacher in a movie called *My Science Project*. It was a Touchstone Films production, and Touchstone is part of Walt Disney Studios. Of all places for Hopper to find work, that was the last one he, or anyone else, had expected. He had to laugh at the irony of the notorious bad boy doing a movie for a company known for its wholesome, squeaky-clean image. He said, "It's something I never thought would happen, but the role offered me an opportunity to return to filmmaking in Los Angeles. Before *My Science Project*, I hadn't worked on a Hollywood sound stage in over twenty years. I wanted the part. I'm anxious to work."

The role turned out to be a lark for Dennis. He played an ex-hippie science teacher who gets caught in a space-time warp. He comes out looking like Hopper's *Easy Rider* character, Billy. "It's a real gag. I'm right out of the Sixties, spouting the same rhetoric like 'Hell no, I won't go,' 'flower power,' and I even get carted off to jail. It was, well, sort of déjà vu," Hopper commented. It was as though Dennis was announcing to the entire movie industry that he was killing off that character for good, with laughter, and was ready to get on with life in the 1980s.

It was a successful reintroduction to Hollywood filmmaking for Dennis. He was on his way to building a new reputation for himself. He next did a movie for television in which he played a supporting role as a Las Vegas police officer in *Stark*. He came across believably as the old-style, straight-down-the-line cop, doing it by the numbers, the foil for a younger, maverick detective who solves the mystery by breaking the rules. As Dennis had said a few years before, it was time for him to make the transition from being the son to the father. Years before it would have been Hopper in the role of the rebellious detective. Now he was being asked to play authority figures like teachers and tradition-bound police lieutenants.

People in Hollywood started to take notice. Rumors of an entirely different sort began circulating about Hopper. Those who were acquainted with him and his past antics incredulously asked one another, "Have you heard, do you think it's on the level? They say he's gone straight—no booze, no drugs." They saw him on screen and he looked great—tan, trim, fit, and clear-eyed. They started seeing him around town and he appeared to be in top-notch form. It seemed too good to be true, but he was proving the doubters wrong. Dennis said, "My sobriety is something that's showing the industry that they can accept me and count on me. I don't have the mood swings, I don't have the messy personal life that I had."

By early 1985 he was eagerly looking for work. He was ready to say yes to any projects that came his way. He even picked up his cameras again and did a layout on his homes in Taos and Los Angeles for *Vanity Fair* magazine. It was the first photographic work he had done since he put down his equipment to sit in the director's chair on *Easy Rider*. There was interest in him coming from all over. A publisher approached him about putting out a book of his photographs from the Sixties. Music legends Phil Spector and Bob Dylan were talking to him about directing their music videos. Meanwhile, he had already performed in a special fifty-minute music video for Mick Jagger, playing the part of an American director, a role he hoped to play in real life again in the near future.

He still believed in his baby, *The Last Movie*. In the spring of 1985 he took it to France for its first showing at the Cannes Film Festival. The reception at Cannes was enthusiastic and he left France with a tentative European distribution deal for his film at long last, though it was unfortunately destined to fall through. He returned to Hollywood to discuss a deal to play the role of a geologist in *Two Jakes*, the troubled sequel to *Chinatown* that has been rumored to be in the works for years. He was also enthusiastically touting a sequel to *Easy Rider*, which he referred to as *Biker's Heaven*. He said it would take some big financing because it was set two hundred years after a nuclear holocaust and the script called for a lot of special effects. He and Peter Fonda and Jack Nicholson would reprise their roles from *Easy Rider*. When reminded that they had all died in the original, Hopper said, "Yeah. It's a black comedy."

By the end of May he was traveling again, headed for England. *Two Jakes* was not going to happen, again, so he moved on to co-star in *Riders of the Storm* with Michael J. Pollard. Dennis played the captain of a B–29 that had been used in Vietnam, supposedly to disorient the enemy by cutting into all their communications systems with blaring loud rock music. At the end of the war, he and Pollard stole the ship and, as Dennis described it, "We are these crazed guys who have not landed in fifteen years. We've refueled in the air. We are flying somewhere over North America right now with an outlaw video channel that we can use to break in on NBC or CBS, or just give our point of view of the news or play our music and so on. We have this great secret weapon that flies around, dispensing Truth, Justice, and the American Way."

Now the course of his career was building momentum. He rolled from one job into the next. Later in the year he went to Wilmington, North Carolina, to appear in David Lynch's *Blue Velvet*. It was a part he wanted so much he could taste it. Many actors had been vying for the part of psychopathic Frank Booth, even, incredibly, singer Bobby Vinton who had a big hit with the song "Blue Velvet" in the 1950s.

Dennis was on the list for consideration all along, but director David Lynch had misgivings about the legendary rebel: He hadn't heard about the new, improved Dennis Hopper. The one he knew about was the crazed dope fiend who slept with guns. Lynch recalled, "He had been on earlier lists, but because of his reputation, I never really thought about him. But when I heard that he had cleaned up his act, I got real excited. His manager said, 'Look, please talk to the producers who have worked with him recently, they'll tell you he's fantastic.'"

His model behavior was paying off. Lynch checked and found that he was now known for his reliability and cooperative attitude, as well as for being a very talented actor. Dennis clinched the part for himself when he called the director personally and said, "I've got to play this part, David, because I *am* Frank." The joke on the set was that Lynch told the rest of the cast and crew, "My God, he just told me on the phone that he is Frank. I don't know what he meant by that. Maybe he's right for the part, but how are we going to have lunch with him?"

Frank Booth is the villain of *Blue Velvet*, written and directed by Lynch. He is a psychopathic criminal who has kidnapped the husband and child of nightclub singer Dorothy Vallens, played by Isabella Rossellini, the daughter of actress Ingrid Bergman and director Roberto Rossellini. Frank has cut off her husband's ear to prove to her the seriousness of his threats. He has Dorothy in his power so that he can play cruel, sadistic sex games with her, while he inhales some unspecified drug through a mask he holds to his face to heighten the intensity of his experience. Dennis said, "I understand Frank very well. I was known to abuse people when drunk or high, but not exactly in this way. I've also played a lot of sex games. But Dennis Hopper in reality is more a masochist than a sadist."

Frank Booth is pure sadist. He first appears on the screen in one of the most frightening and at the same time sexually charged scenes ever filmed. It fully shows the sadistic relationship he has with Dorothy Vallens. He calls her "Mommy" and insists she call him "Daddy," until he gets sexually aroused, when he becomes "Baby." He excites himself by slapping her into a chair in front of him, with nothing on but her blue velvet robe. She must spread her legs open while he stares at her, and she may not look at him or she is slapped again, until he is sufficiently turned on to engage in brutal intercourse, all the while alternately stuffing the sash of her robe into his mouth and inhaling whatever strange gases or drugs come through the mask he holds over his nose and mouth. Hopper later said he imagined what Frank inhaled through the mask to be an amyl nitrite type of vapor.

Dennis had high praise for Isabella, who was a newcomer to acting. He later said, "She's wonderful. Very like her mother. It's not an affectation, either. She looks a lot like her mother and her voice is like hers, almost identical. She's really a wonderful person and a wonderful actress. She's really very open. We were playing really heavy scenes, I mean heavy!" As Pauline Kael said in her review of the movie in *The New Yorker*, "Isabella Rossellini doesn't show anything like the acting technique that her mother, Ingrid Bergman, had, but she's willing to try things, and she doesn't hold back."

Dennis shared one memorable scene in the movie with his buddy, Dean Stockwell. Stockwell played Ben, the effeminate proprietor of a brothel staffed by overweight prostitutes who sit staring indifferently at the scene unfolding before them, as their boss serenades Frank, lip-synching to the treacly sweet song "In Dreams" by Roy Orbison. His face plastered with pale white makeup so he looks like a perverted version of Pierrot, he moves his lips to the lyrics about "the candy-colored clown they call the sandman." Hopper, as Frank, seems mesmerized at first, then more and more agitated as Ben mouths the words to his favorite song. He gets worked up to the point where he is ready to take Jeffrey, the innocent hero of the film played by Kyle MacLachlan, on a "joy ride" to a secluded spot where Frank and his henchmen beat Jeffrey up. All the while, the saccharine sentimentality of "In Dreams" plays on in the background.

Frank is frighteningly evil, and Dennis played him that way to the hilt, right up to the last moment, when he is gunned down as he is about to murder Jeffrey. He once described the character as "perhaps the most vicious person who has ever been on the screen." And he had played him absolutely straight. He admitted to a reporter that to do that kind of role in the past, "Normally I would have taken cocaine to get that sort of frenzy or I would have used amyl nitrite in the mask."

Instead he had his talent and the help of his director, who urged him to play the part with greater intensity than Hopper had planned to use. He said, "David kept me up really high, pushing all the time. He insisted I keep playing it at a high level." When Dennis saw the final product he said, "I think it's wonderful. I love what I do in the film, and I love what David did with me."

Dennis also called upon the training of his early years in New York with Lee Strasberg in the Actors Studio to take him to the place he needed to be to become Frank and then to go on and play a different, heart-warming character in his next film.

Dennis went directly from filming *Blue Velvet* to Indiana and the set of *Hoosiers*, which starred Gene Hackman and Barbara Hershey. There he spoke with BBC reporter Barbra Paskin at length about the Method. "There were three basic Method teachers. There was Sandy Meisner, who taught Joanne Woodward and Paul Newman and so on. There was Lee Strasberg at the Actors Studio. And there was Stella Adler. Whoever went to Moscow and met Stanislavski came back with their interpretation of what their Method, or their way of approaching work, would be.

"You're basically breaking it down into three things. You have your subconscious, you have your imagination, and you have your senses. And so Stella, who was Marlon's teacher, came back and said everything you can find through the object. If you work with the object, it will make your imagination happen and your senses will be affected and you will reach your subconscious. So use objects. You'll notice when Brando acts, he is always working with objects of one kind or another. So this is one way you can break down and reach your subconscious.

"Meisner," Dennis continued, "said it's your imagination. You get your imagination working properly, it will stimulate your senses and by stimulating your senses you will reach your subconscious. Like little kids playing in a field: 'Bang, bang, you're dead.' 'No, you missed me.' 'Yeah, I got you.'

"Strasberg said it's the senses. If you develop your senses through sense memory and then go into emotional memory, then your imagination will work and you will reach your subconscious."

Dennis expanded his theme further: "Because the hardest thing in the world is first to be in front of an audience, but then to reach your subconscious through a conscious means is almost impossible. I mean, you can say, 'Oh my God. My mother, when she died, or when my father died—' But it has no meaning to your subconscious. Thinking about the very fact they died does not bring on any sorrow or any emotion that you felt at the time that this actually happened.

"So you have to trick yourself through asking, 'What was I wearing?' or not 'What was I wearing?' but 'Can I feel what I was wearing that day, was it hot that day, can I feel some of that heat? The sound, what was I hearing?' And through that, rather than relating to the incident, you can then trick your subconscious into reacting, through whatever given sense. And then you can do your scene."

Dennis had to call on his Method training while filming *Hoosiers* to be able to achieve the great believability he reached in several drunk scenes he had. He played the part of Shooter Flagg, the town drunk in a small rural Indiana community that lives and breathes basketball during the 1950s. Director David Anspaugh and screenwriter–co-producer Angelo Pizzo, both Indiana native sons who conceived the idea for the picture when they were college fraternity brothers, had based their story of fictional Hickory High School's basketball victory on the true story of rural Milan High, which went all the way to the top in the 1954 Indiana state basketball championship.

Hopper, too, scored a triumph in this movie. For a complete change from his *Blue Velvet* character, he played an essentially likeable man with a big problem that he tries to overcome during the course of the film. And the movie itself was different from most of his others. People left the theater feeling good after watching *Hoosiers*, emotionally recharged on the uplifting ending.

The story is of a mediocre small-town basketball team that is transformed into true champions through the loving but tough discipline of the new coach, who is hiding out at the high-school level, having disgraced himself at his last job coaching a college team. He was banned from coaching at the university level for having hit one of his players when his usually well-controlled but explosive temper burst to the surface during a crucial game. Hackman played the new coach, and Barbara Hershey played the high-school teacher who is at first antagonistic to the new coach because she values education over basketball, but ends up falling in love with him because he is such a decent man in spite of his flaws.

Hopper played a crucial supporting character, Shooter Flagg. He is a man who had one chance at glory in his own high-school days, but blew it when he missed the winning shot at the basketball championship played many years ago.

His life since then has been on a downward spiral and now he is the town drunk, the butt of everyone's jokes and a humiliation to his son, who to some degree follows in his father's footsteps by playing on the high-school basketball team.

Coach Dale gives Shooter an opportunity for redemption. Shooter goes to all the basketball games and has an extensive knowledge of the strengths and weaknesses of all the area high-school teams. He starts out coming by late at night to give scouting reports to the coach. Then when the high-school principal, Dale's old buddy who has been acting as assistant coach, has an incapacitating heart attack, the coach offers Shooter the position over the objections of the entire town, but only if he promises to stay sober. The plan works for a few games, with some backsliding, but Shooter shows up at a crucial semifinal game, stoned out of his gourd, lurching onto the court and completely disrupting the game. Dennis has a great scene to play here, as the wildly drunk man completely embarrasses his son, who injures himself in a fight ensuing from his father's humiliating entrance.

After this final disgrace, Shooter ends up in a hospital detoxification unit for treatment of his alcoholism. The original script had called for Shooter to break out of the detox ward and show up at the final championship game to see the team to victory. However, that did not sit well with Dennis's newfound principles. As a recovering alcoholic, it was not the kind of message he wanted to convey.

He later told a reporter, "Being an alcoholic, I felt that it was really destructive to have Shooter leave. Maybe he'll never get sober, but he ain't going to get sober if he goes to that game. I said, 'Just do a shot of me in the hospital jumping up and down while listening to the game on the radio.' I sacrificed a lot of movie time up there on the screen." But he also gained for himself a very effective scene that showed everything it was important for his character to demonstrate: his commitment to basketball and to the team and his pride in his son. And it had the added bonus of offering hope that Shooter would straighten himself out and give his son a father to be proud of.

On the other hand, Dennis harbored no illusions that his portrayal of Shooter would necessarily make a difference in another alcoholic's life, no matter how great a performance he gave. He said, "I know about how to be a drunk real well. I don't think it probably helps anyone that Shooter ends up in treatment, because unfortunately most drunks are charming, devious people. So I don't know that it helps anyone to see what happens to him, except that he's a terrible embarrassment to his son and he's hurting people around him—and he's hurting himself." He might almost have been speaking of his own past with those words.

When asked what had appealed to him about the role to begin with, Dennis answered, "I liked it on a number of levels. I thought it was a nice little part, that it had charm to it. It had a certain beginning, middle, and an end to it, that the character was rather realized in its own way. I also like the fact that it was an alcoholic who ended up in treatment, because that is what happened to me three years ago. . . . I bottomed out, and my character bottoms out in this and is put into treatment.

"And," he continued, "I liked the idea of working with Gene Hackman." Hopper later joked that he and Hackman had been puzzled by the director and screenwriter's insistence on filming "all those damned basketball games. We were sitting on these wooden benches saying, 'Here's the big money. Why aren't you shooting us?'"

Hopper recalled the extent of his basketball involvement before *Hoosiers* for reporters at the premiere of the film in Indiana. "When I was growing up in Kansas, we had a hoop over the barn," he remembered. And now, "Well, I go to the Lakers games with my friend Jack," he said, referring to buddy Jack Nicholson, an avid basketball fan and a regular courtside at Los Angeles Lakers games.

On the serious side, Dennis appreciated the difficult task director David Anspaugh had chosen for himself. While on the set of *Hoosiers* he told reporter Barbra Paskin, "I think that what we're doing right now is really difficult because of all the young guys and the basketball games." The youngsters who played the members of the team were experienced basketball players but not actors. "I mean, you read a half a page or so of the script and it describes a basketball game, but in reality what you're doing is like ten days of shooting to get the shots and the coverage and so on. I just think David's doing fine.

"I don't need a lot of help as an actor and Gene doesn't need a lot of help as an actor, and I appreciate it when we're just sort of left alone. I don't find that nondirecting; I find it just appreciation. I find David is doing well. I think he's got a really tough assignment, which he's made for himself, obviously, since this is his own script. He's doing fine."

The public certainly agreed. They loved *Hoosiers* and proved it at the box office. It was a crowd pleaser that put Dennis Hopper's name in front of a much wider public than *Blue Velvet*, with all its strangeness, was able to. Many critics felt the highlight of *Hoosiers* was Hopper's supporting performance as Shooter. One critic described Dennis in the film as "not always standing but damned near running away with the picture," stealing scenes from the magnetic Hackman. He was equally affecting in scenes showing him struggling to hold on to sobriety as in those he drunkenly staggered and slurred his way through. A touching moment in the hospital between Shooter and his son, Ray, rings loud and true when he says, "I feel real empty inside, and I have some bad visions." To look at Hopper's face at that moment is to look at a man who has felt that emptiness and seen the horrors lurking there.

Was Hopper playing himself again, as downplayers of his talents had often claimed? Perhaps, but to be able to focus his personal experiences and his own feelings sharply enough to put them across on the movie screen to an audience is one of Hopper's greatest acting achievements. It is something that he has dared to do time and again, with an honesty that is almost brutal to himself. This time it was worth it. He was not doing it in a film that would die a discreet death in art-film houses. His performance in *Hoosiers* would earn him ample recognition from the public, from critics, and from his peers in the acting community.

CHAPTER FOURTEEN

Nineteen eighty-six looked like the year of Dennis Hopper. By April he would be able to look back on two years of complete sobriety and three years without a drink. Over the course of twenty-four months he had appeared in almost as many films as he had worked on in the fifteen years prior, when he was still hung up on drugs and booze. And there was no end of work in sight, just a harvest to be reaped for having sown the seeds of his own spiritual renewal.

His outstanding performances in *Blue Velvet* and *Hoosiers* had not been seen by the public yet, but his new reputation was growing in the film industry. He could look back over the many months since he had emerged from Cedars-Sinai psychiatric ward and say, "In a year and a half I've had maybe a week off. That's good. It's disastrous for an actor, or a director, to sit around thinking about why he isn't working. Bills don't stop."

And Dennis was piling up the bills since he had decided to come back to Hollywood. When he made up his mind to leave Taos behind for good and move to Los Angeles, he said, "I was trying to decide where I'd live. I hated Los Angeles, but I had good memories of Venice." He remembered when he was eighteen and he and Jimmy Dean would go to Venice to hear the Beat poets reciting their works, backed up by cool jazz.

The town of Venice outside of Santa Monica held additional appeal for him because it was also home to many artists, some of them Hopper's friends. Besides its colony of artists, the beach community is also known for the bitter black versus Latino teenage-gang rivalry, which often bursts into violence. As for the occasional gunshots punctuating the nights: "I don't mind it—I kind of like it," Dennis remarked flippantly. Venice is not a glamorous community, but the small population of artists, directors, and actors who live there in *Architectural Digest*-worthy homes interspersed among the stucco apartment buildings and dilapidated bungalows gives it a cachet nearly equal to its northerly neighbor, Malibu.

He bought a condominium that had originally been designed to be an artist's studio, on the border of a neighborhood known as the War Zone, a part of Venice rife with gang violence. The inside had an intentionally unfinished look so that it was a bit like living in a lumberyard. Dennis worked closely with a designer to keep that raw, industrial look. A lot of the structural elements were left exposed and an unfinished wood staircase led up to a sleeping loft where Dennis had installed Mexican Day of the Dead skeleton statues, dressed in carnival clothes, who were posed as though engaged in a sword fight. His quirky eye for home decorating hadn't changed since he and Brooke Hayward had shared their West Hollywood home.

Not long after he took up residence, Dennis realized the

1,200-square-foot condo would just not be big enough, especially once he was sharing it with his girlfriend and production assistant, Jamie Thompson. They were squeezed in with all the big pieces of carved oak Spanish furniture and neoclassical French sofas he had carted off from the Mabel Dodge Luhan mansion, plus the art he was starting to collect again. Most of the paintings remained rolled up while he decided what to do. He liked the neighborhood and he liked what the designer he worked with, Brian Murphy, had done to the interior of the condominium, so he bought an adjacent vacant lot and asked Murphy to design a larger house. He would keep the condo for a guest house.

Murphy designed a modernistic fortress for a contemporary romantic warrior, though Dennis would call it "a major studio for a minor artist." The front of the house is surfaced in corrugated iron, the front door studded with bolts. The four front windows, two on either side of the forbidding entrance, are barred. An elaborate network of security systems includes one that flashes all the lights in the house on and off if it detects the slightest false move. Dennis had chosen to live in the War Zone, but he wanted it to stay out there, not intrude on the house which is ironically surrounded by a white picket fence, much like the one seen with red roses in front in the opening scenes of *Blue Velvet*.

The new house had plenty of living space and it incorporated work areas as well. He had a studio for his own painting and photography. There were areas especially designed to display his collection of work by other artists. He also got enough room for a small theater that could double as a teaching space, in case he ever stopped his own work long enough to give acting classes.

However, at this point there was plenty of employment to keep him out of the classroom. He appeared in a television movie called *Stark: Mirror Image*, a sequel to the *Stark* movie he had done in 1985, reprising the role of Las Vegas police Lieutenant Ron Bliss. The straight-arrow Bliss contrasted sharply with his next outing on the big screen, a sociopathic character called Feck that he tackled in a movie called *River's Edge.*

This film offered an even darker portrait of American youth than Hopper had shown in his own *Out of the Blue.* In *River's Edge,* a crowd of teenagers, whose main extracurricular activity is getting stoned, are confronted with a murder committed by one of their friends and find themselves at a loss, morally, as to how to behave. Instead of reporting the killing, they conspire to conceal the young girl's corpse and shield their friend from detection.

The part of Feck gave Dennis the chance to ring the death knell for the hippie character of the Sixties that still clung to his image like the lingering smell of marijuana smoke. Through this role he could show how bankrupt the philosophy represented by that persona had become. Feck is a burned-out biker the kids usually buy their pot from. This is how Billy of *Easy Rider* easily might have turned out. He lives in isolation with his inflatable sex doll named Ellie. The teenagers turn to him for advice when figuring out how to help the murderer in their midst, and he fascinates them by speaking romantically of killing a girl he once loved. Hopper twitched and giggled his way through *River's Edge,* which he later said he preferred to *Blue Velvet,* though he considered both to be great movies. He felt *Blue Velvet* was somewhat naive in its point of view while *River's Edge* had something more to it. As he explained: "I liked *River's Edge* a lot. . . . It's not my best work—I don't like the way my performance was edited in it. But the film is unique, and real frightening. I find it scarier than *Blue Velvet. Blue Velvet* lets you off. You get some humor once in a while where you can breathe and say, 'Well, it's a movie.' There's something about *River's Edge* that gets me. The apathy of the characters I find really scary."

171

Dennis went on to do another "scary" movie that he did not have to take seriously, but it was employment that kept the cash coming in. He spent part of the spring of 1986 in Austin, Texas, on the horror film *Texas Chainsaw Massacre, Part 2*, taking the role of an avenging sheriff in pursuit of the chainsaw murderers. He later gave his own critique of the film, saying, "I was lousy—it's a lousy film, but I had fun doing it." He enjoyed the fairly relaxed shooting schedule, which included a lot of time off for him.

While on the *Texas Chainsaw* location, Dennis's fiftieth birthday came and really caught him off guard. As a young man he had thought of fifty as over the hill and washed up. He had thought a fifty-year-old was somebody who should be ready to step aside and let the young lions take over. It hadn't seemed real to him that he might someday reach that age. Yet, here he was at the half-century mark feeling more alive and full of energy than he'd felt in ages, with renewed plans to make his mark on the art and film worlds.

In April he had been so happy to celebrate his second year since his rebirth, completely free of substance abuse, that he hadn't focused on his chronological birthday coming up in May. They surprised him on the film set by rolling out a huge cake bordered with fifty candles. Then someone handed Dennis, appropriately enough, a chainsaw. Laughing, Dennis posed for photographs with the blade poised over the cake to cut the first slice.

The highlight for him, however, was taking a day away from the set to spend his birthday with country-western singer Willie Nelson. They played in Nelson's golf invitational at the Pederales Country Club, and Dennis went home with the second-place trophy.

As for turning fifty, Dennis was reported to say, "I thought I'd be dead before I was thirty. Turning forty stunned me. Fifty is a major miracle, and I think I may even make seventy."

People in the film industry continued to consider Dennis for supporting roles, not for leads. No one was sure yet whether he could carry a picture on his own, though given half a chance he might steal it out from under a weaker leading actor. The situation was frustrating to Dennis, but he had a lot more patience now than he did as a young man when he went running away to New Mexico to sulk when things didn't go his way quickly enough. If he had to prove himself further, he would keep on churning out gems of supporting performances for as long as it took to convince the industry that he was really back and better than ever.

Besides, what he wanted more than a good leading role was another crack at directing. He was constantly looking at scripts and story ideas, looking for a deal he could put together that would allow him to get behind the cameras again. Meanwhile, there was another picture in preparation, produced by his old friend Warren Beatty. The role offered him seemed all too familiar to Dennis—another in his series of alcoholic fathers. Hopper was available and not in the mood to turn down any offers of work, especially not one that came from Warren Beatty, an actor who had leveraged himself into a powerful position in Hollywood, where he was sought after as an actor, free to direct with artistic control, and able to launch his own productions.

The Beatty production, *The Pick Up Artist*, starred Molly Ringwald, one of the hottest young actresses around, who while still in her teens had appeared in box office smash after smash. Hopper's part did have a new twist to it: This time he was an alcoholic father with a gambling problem. Unfortunately, Ringwald's box office magic didn't rub off on *The Pick Up Artist*. The reviews were negative and the film faded quickly from the theaters when it was released the following summer.

Before the fate of his film was known, director James Toback spoke of how younger actors could look up to Hopper as a veteran of the Hollywood scene, one who did not spout hypocritical warnings or advice. "He's a good spirit to hang around on the set," Toback reported, and went on to say, "He's one of the few people who has gone through those [rehabilitation] programs and has cleaned out his system internally and externally, and yet he is not at all a proselytizer or a voice of doom. Which is frequently the case with former degenerates who have reformed."

Hopper was not sure how to take the admiration, and felt puzzled when youngsters asked him for advice. He said, "I find this amusing. I hear things like, 'They're so impressed that you're here.' I find it so bizarre, I can't connect with it."

Hopper did reciprocate the admiration of some of the new generation of actors he had already worked with. He particularly praised two of the young men who had co-starred in *River's Edge*. He said, "I see a lot of good actors around. Daniel Roebuck [who played the murderer] from *River's Edge* is a good actor, and he's only twenty-two." He went on to compare Crispin Glover, who played the ringleader in *River's Edge* and had also played the part of Michael J. Fox's father in *Back to the Future*, to James Dean, saying, "Crispin does such strange things, almost like a dancer. Jimmy was like that." Expanding on his meaning, Dennis said, "This is at a time in the Fifties when actors only did the script. But Jimmy did the script and then some. Like in *Rebel Without a Cause*, when they arrest him for being drunk and disorderly, they start searching him and he starts laughing like they're tickling him. He was doing things you don't really see—except for maybe Crispin Glover."

He also admired the work of a young man he had not performed with: Sean Penn. Sean and his wife, pop singer and actress Madonna, had high regard for Dennis's acting, but were particularly interested in his work as a director. They were fans of *Out of the Blue*. Early in their marriage, the Penns had appeared in one movie together, *Shanghai Surprise*, a comedy-adventure that turned out to be neither funny nor exciting. It flopped resoundingly with the critics and at the box office. The Penns were searching for another property to appear in together and were eager that Hopper be the one to direct them.

Dennis was familiar with and impressed with Sean's past screen performances, and he wasn't turned off by the young actor's "bad boy" image played up by the press. Hopper was all too aware of what the slightest bit of uncooperative behavior could do to a young man in Hollywood. He fully empathized with Sean, having been the victim of bad publicity for much of his own career. He may even have seen in Sean a bit of himself as a younger man, or the ghost of Jimmy popping up again in the next generation.

Madonna and Sean Penn met with Dennis to get acquainted and talk in general ways about working together. There was no specific project to discuss, but the meeting went well. Before the Penns left, Dennis noticed that Sean was reading a book by Charles Bukowski, a poet and novelist famed for his alcoholic excesses and bowery bum life-style. Dennis asked Sean if he was an admirer of Bukowski. When Sean replied that he was, Dennis said, "I know a Bukowski property called *Barfly* that you should do, that you'd be perfect for the lead in, that Barbet Schroeder had Bukowski write for him as a screenplay."

Penn was definitely interested, but only if Hopper could direct. He told Sean, "There's no way to get this from Barbet Schroeder—I ended up enemies with him when I told him he couldn't direct traffic."

But the young actor got a copy of the script, read it, and fell in love with it. He went directly to Bukowski to tell him how much he liked the screenplay and yearned to play the part. From the time he had written it in 1979, Bukowski had been doubtful that anything would ever happen with the story. He had been skeptical when Schroeder asked him to author it, wondering what movie executive would stick his neck out to make a film about a hopeless drunk. Bukowski himself said, "Barbet tried to palm it off on everyone. He'd get these notes from producers saying, 'Sure, it's good, but who cares about a drunk?'"

No one did, until Sean Penn started to show interest in it. Bukowski, whose nickname is Hank, reported that Sean said to him, "'Hank, I'll act in it for a dollar. That'll be my salary.' Suddenly people started perking up, figuring if Sean Penn wanted to act in it for a dollar, well, there must be something in there for somebody."

But it was still Schroeder's property. Penn was stubbornly loyal to Hopper, whose work he so admired and who had been the one to turn him on to *Barfly* to begin with. Bukowski would not consider cutting out his patron, Schroeder, who had waited so long and patiently, now that it looked like the script had a chance of actually being made into a movie. Bukowski decided some action was needed to move away from this impasse, so he invited the two would-be directors and the young star to meet at his house in San Pedro, down by the Los Angeles harbor.

"It was a great meeting," Bukowski later reported. "Schroeder and Hopper had been enemies for centuries, ever since Dennis had told Barbet that he couldn't direct traffic. I got the drinks out, for everyone except Dennis, who's straight now. But Barbet had already built such a case against Dennis that by the time he walked in the door I was ready to cut his throat. I think he was nervous; he laughed too much, tried too hard."

Dennis said later, "We had a meeting in which Bukowski said no to me. He wanted Sean to do it really badly, with Barbet, but Sean said, 'Unless Dennis directs, I'm not going to do it.'"

It was a lost cause to try to change Bukowski's mind. He would not budge from his loyalty to Schroeder, Penn refused to take the lead without Hopper, but enough interest had been stirred up in Hollywood that the picture was made and released in 1987, with Mickey Rourke taking over the starring role, and, of course, Barbet Schroeder directing.

Dennis had not held much hope for getting the *Barfly* script away from Schroeder and had continued negotiating another deal to direct that did not involve Sean Penn or Madonna. Meanwhile, he made a brief cameo appearance in *Black Widow*, playing a Texas toy-manufacturing tycoon who is one of Theresa Russell's early husband-victims, knocked off by a toxin injected into his bottle of Remy Martin. He took the tiny part as a favor to director Bob Rafelson, another old friend who had been instrumental in getting financial backing for *Easy Rider*, when he co-produced Dennis's long-ago directorial debut.

Now, nearly twenty years later, Dennis looked forward to directing again. September 1986 found him in Philadelphia, scouting locations for a movie called *Marked for Life*. Dennis was going to direct only; he would not appear as an actor in the drama about four boys who tattoo themselves as an expression of their undying loyalty and friendship in 1944. One goes to prison for twenty-one years and, when he is released, finds his friends still expect his unchanged allegiance. Sadly, as Dennis had experienced the first time he was set to direct *The Last Movie*, the financial backing for the picture fell through before filming could begin.

Luckily Dennis did not have much time on his hands to lament that *Marked for Life* had fallen through. He knew that too many days of unemployment, spent self-indulgently

177

dwelling on why he couldn't direct that movie, could lead him right back to a place he had struggled very hard to get away from. Every day was still a fight to stay out of the wasteland. He remembered his own words: "It's disastrous for an actor or a director to sit around thinking about why he isn't working."

He went right to work again, acting in a movie called *Blood Red*, a historical drama in which he played an Irish railroad builder who goes up against Italian grape growers. Of his part, Dennis said, "Let's just say I'm a man who takes care of business."

By the end of 1986, the general moviegoing public got to see how Dennis Hopper, the actor, had been taking care of business. *Blue Velvet* was released in the fall, and *Hoosiers* in December. Talk of an Academy Award nomination for Best Supporting Actor for Dennis began circulating as soon as the critics laid eyes on his knockout performance in *Hoosiers*. Many reviewers also liked *Blue Velvet* and his performance in it, but it wasn't a mainstream, mass-appeal movie like *Hoosiers*.

The end of 1986 and beginning of 1987 brought Dennis a flurry of awards and nominations for Best Supporting Actor of 1986 for his performances in both films. He won the National Society of Film Critics honor for Best Supporting Actor in *Blue Velvet* and *Hoosiers*; the Los Angeles Film Critics association also gave him the Best Supporting Actor award for both. He won the Best Actor award for *Blue Velvet* at the Montreal Film Festival. For the Golden Globe Awards, he was nominated in the Supporting Actor category for both films but lost to Tom Berenger, who won for his performance in *Platoon*, one of the blockbuster films of 1986.

While he received numerous awards and nominations for his performance as psychopathic Frank Booth in *Blue*

Velvet, it was Shooter Flagg that won the hearts of his fellow actors who nominated him for an Academy Award in the Best Supporting Actor category for 1986. Shooter had won the hearts of the public as well.

Dennis could laugh about people's varying reactions to the two films that had brought him back into the limelight. He said, "Since *Hoosiers* opened, people have been coming up to me and saying, 'I loved you in that movie.' And I can tell from their faces that it's not *Blue Velvet* they're talking about. People come up and say 'that movie' about *Blue Velvet*, too, but they have fear in their eyes. If they reach out at all, it's with somebody in front of them. They peer around and say, 'God, you were great in that movie.'" He knew the work he had done was good, and it pleased him to get public recognition for it.

Nineteen eighty-seven was shaping up to be even better than 1986. By the time the Academy Award nominations were announced in February 1987, Dennis had more to celebrate than the Best Supporting Actor nomination. He was really going to direct again. All the contracts had been signed, the financing was sewn up; this was the real thing.

Dennis and Sean Penn had continued searching for a vehicle for Dennis to direct and Sean to star in. Sean had found a script about cops and drug dealers that he brought to Dennis. Dennis set to work on it. He liked the basic concept, but there were some major problems with the original story. "I ripped the script apart, which was set in Chicago. They were dealing in cough syrup, and there was this big bust that saved the world from this cough syrup dealing. It was total bullshit." Dennis suggested some changes: Move the action to Los Angeles, focus on the central characters, an older cop and a younger cop, and show how they interact, make it about the reality of gangs who are dealing in heroin, cocaine, and PCP.

Dennis said the initial response to his changes was,

"'Nobody wants to see that stuff,' and I said, 'They don't want to see anything about *cough syrup*! And you don't have one bust and save everybody from street gangs.'"

Sean believed wholeheartedly in Dennis and refused to sign on for his role until Dennis held in his hands a signed contract to direct the film. Dennis was deeply impressed with the integrity of the younger actor, and was reminded of his own old battles with the establishment for artistic honesty.

Dennis felt on top of the world on a brisk day in January 1987. He confidently wheeled his two-tone tan Cadillac Seville east from his home in Venice. (Somewhat embarrassed by his choice of vehicle, he once excused it by explaining to a reporter who was riding with him that he bought it when he was so high on drugs he thought it was some kind of tank.) He was a far cry from the man who had come out of a psychiatric ward afraid to drive Bert Schneider's car to his psychiatrist's office. He drove to Century City to meet with Orion Pictures executives Mike Medavoy and Eric Pleskow. Even the kidding he took from the movie bigwigs about how straight he looked in his suit and tie, carrying a briefcase, could not perturb him. Sean Penn had signed his contract and Pleskow and Medavoy had called Dennis in for a meeting to give him the go-ahead to begin directing his fourth film in February.

When the whole deal was finalized, Penn was set to co-star with Hopper's old friend Robert Duvall and Latin American beauty Maria Conchita Alonso in a movie called *Colors*. The movie would be Dennis's first feature filmed using an all-union crew; he would finally be inducted into the Director's Guild of America.

Dennis had his work cut out for him on *Colors*. He had to deal with the strong personalities of Penn and Duvall as well as keep a tight rein over his own emotions so that the film did not go off track.

He and Sean had done a lot of preparation before the shooting got under way. The Los Angeles police permitted them to accompany their youth-gang experts on duty, to observe the reality of cops versus street gangs. They were both familiar with sitting in the backseats of police cars, but being welcomed guests of the fuzz was a brand new experience. Hopper and Penn became experts at deciphering the cryptic graffiti spray-painted on walls all over L.A., declaring each gang's turf, warning off rivals, or challenging the homeboys.

Most of the location shooting was on Dennis's home turf in Venice. It was an obvious choice because of the amount of gang activity in the area, but it also gave Dennis a lot of control over the shooting schedule. He was so familiar with the neighborhood that he could plan shots with the minimum amount of moving the big movie crew around. He remembered everything he had learned on all his previous directing assignments, and this time he brought something more to the director's chair: a clear head.

As fellow director James Toback said of him, "He's probably in a very good frame of mind to direct now. There's a point beyond which it becomes clear that every act might be your last. I think that he already feels that he's living on borrowed time. There were X-number of occasions when he could just as well have died as lived. All of a sudden you get a chance to direct a movie again, and it's a gift."

Hopper knew he would be a much better director now that he was sober, just as he was a better actor since he had gained more control over himself. He said, "It will be a much clearer image than I've ever given before because alcohol and drugs, when they work, may give you bursts of creative energy but you get sloppy and the result is not a clear and sober picture. . . . You can't lie to yourself when you're straight."

Dennis was staying straight, but he feared that one of his stars might land in jail before they finished the film. Penn had earned himself a reputation as a young man with a fiery temper. He was alleged to have gone after reporters and photographers with rocks and fists when they approached him. There were pictures of him spitting at photographers. And he was prone to jealousy over his wife. There was ample opportunity for his jealous nature to be ignited, being married to Madonna, one of the most popular sex symbols of the pop music scene.

Sean was facing a court appearance in February, just as they were beginning to film *Colors*. David Wolinski, a musician friend of Madonna's, had pressed charges against Penn for attacking him when he had met the singer by chance at Helena's, an exclusive Los Angeles nightclub, back in April 1986. Sean reportedly assaulted Wolinski in a jealous rage when he thought the musician had kissed his wife.

Dennis was relieved when Sean's hearing was over. His star pleaded no contest to the charge when he appeared in a Los Angeles courtroom and was released but placed on one year's probation. Now Penn needed to walk the straight and narrow. All it would take was one violation and he could wind up facing real jail time if he wasn't careful. And Sean did not impress his older friend as the careful type.

In spite of the twenty-five-year difference in their ages, he and Sean had a lot in common. Dennis had lived through personal rough times like Sean was still experiencing. They also shared a total dedication to their art. Sean was the type of actor who would live a role. People who worked with him on the film that was his big break, *Fast Times at Ridgemont High*, reported that he stayed in character even when the cameras were off, and insisted that everyone call him Jeff, the character's name. The director of that film, Amy Heckerling, said after the film was over, "I kind of know Sean, but I really just know Jeff Spicoli." That kind of commitment to acting and the honesty Sean brought to every part were traits that Dennis could closely identify with.

While Sean was doing fine as an actor, the way his personal life was going might lead to disaster. Dennis could have tried to warn Sean off the path he was following, but he was no preacher. There was no way to talk to the younger man about it—Dennis wouldn't have listened when he was Sean's age either. So he just watched and kept his fingers crossed, hoping to get his film in the can before the Penn temper flared up and got the leading man into more trouble.

Hopper was in total control on the set, displaying the tactical skills of a general in getting final takes on film as quickly as possible, keeping the crew and his actors working all the time. There was no wasted movement or excess fat on his project. He had won his director's seat slogging through the Peruvian mud and shivering in Canada, working on tight budgets and tighter schedules. He may have been stoned then, but he hadn't forgotten what he learned on those earlier films. He had no intention of blowing it now that he had a more generous budget, a trained union crew, and the luxury of a ten-week shooting schedule.

A member of the crew said that the consensus of everyone who worked on *Colors* was: "Dennis is great. He's really talented and skilled. At the same time, he's just a regular guy and treated everyone like fellow workers, equal partners in making the movie. There were no problems, as long as they were doing their jobs.

"He wouldn't stand for anyone shirking, not pulling their weight. Sure, he got angry sometimes, but there was really no trouble on the set. There's a lot of respect out there for Dennis.

"He is completely straight now. He really doesn't do any drugs, booze, nothing like that, unless you want to count the cigarettes. The pressure was getting to him sometimes, you could tell, and then he'd be chain-smoking. Other than that, he's totally clean."

Dennis *needed* a clear head to direct *Colors*; he was filming many scenes on location in parts of Los Angeles that are plagued by real-life gang activity. And never one to take the easy way out, he took the additional risk of using real L.A. gang members as extras, in spite of warnings from gang-behavior experts, working as technical advisers on the film, who counseled that mixing gangs, cops, and movie people on one set would create a volatile, uncontrollable situation. Dennis recalled the day one hundred and forty "gang-bangers" arrived at Lionsgate Studios for their interviews and auditions: "It scared everybody at the studio. The cops said they'd never seen so many gang kids in one location in their lives."

Without bloodshed about twenty gang members were chosen to work on *Colors*. The technical advisers took care that the youngsters chosen were "clean kids"—in gangs but not on probation. A Los Angeles County probation officer said, "We thought it would be good for the kids to see another side of the story, to see people getting paid for doing a real job." By the time the film opened, it was clear that for at least two of the young men their brush with Hollywood and legal employment may have come too late: One was awaiting trial on charges he had murdered a rival gang member and another had been picked up for possession of a deadly weapon. On the other hand, the probation officer said, "One of the kids was in and out of jail almost every week, and now he's making some honest money and has stayed out of jail since the film."

With Sean Penn already on probation, it was ironic that the film's advisers were so careful to choose only gang members who were "clean" to work on *Colors*.

As for Penn's reputation for being a difficult character to deal with, Hopper countered that by quoting his co-star from *Hoosiers*, saying, "Gene Hackman said to me, 'Most people who have any talent are difficult to handle. Otherwise, they are just pleasing people—people pleasers—and they don't usually have very much talent.' I'm not sure," Dennis continued, "that Sean Penn is difficult to deal with. I don't find him difficult to deal with."

Dennis gave high marks to both stars of his film. He said, "Sean and Duvall go toe to toe, and they're both incredible and need very little direction. Just set the camera and let them go. It was a wonderful experience. We never had an argument. Duvall went away saying this was the greatest experience he'd ever had." For Duvall it was a 180-degree difference from his experience years ago with his and Hopper's mutual nemesis, director Henry Hathaway on *True Grit*.

Dennis praised the younger actor further when he said, "Sean Penn is the most professional actor I've ever worked with in my entire life. I don't know a better young actor. He may not be the most handsome young actor, but he's the best. Sean doesn't want any press, he just wants to do his work. Montgomery Clift, Marlon Brando, James Dean— they never gave interviews. The myths around them were set up by the press. That's not uncommon in the history of our media."

Since Hopper was speaking to the press, he had to spend quite a bit of time defending young Penn, especially after Dennis's worst nightmare came true. It happened at the beginning of April, after about seven weeks of filming on the *Colors* location in Venice. Jeffrey Klein, a movie extra, approached Sean during a break. He had a camera he had been using to capture remembrances of his moviemaking experience. Dennis later said Sean had asked Klein to keep the camera away from him. "Sean said, 'Please don't take my picture. I'm working,'" Hopper recalled. There were reports that the man persisted in taking photos, then spit at the young actor, which made Sean go berserk. Sean slugged the extra and tried to smash the camera. Other people on the set stepped between the two men to stop any further violence.

The specter of his film being shut down loomed in front

of Dennis. He told a reporter, "It almost stopped the picture. Sean has to go to court and he could go to prison. It's getting a little out of hand." Dennis was right. Since Penn was already on probation because of the earlier incident in the nightclub, he had landed in a serious spot. Luckily for Hopper's film, by the time Sean had to appear in court, the *Colors* shoot was finished. Penn had meanwhile been picked up for drunk driving, though the charge was reduced to reckless driving because it was his first driving offense. On his day in court, he was sentenced to sixty days in jail, which he served in two separate stints, broken by a trip to Germany to appear in a film his father, Leo Penn, was directing.

If there was any career disappointment in 1987 for Hopper, it was losing the Oscar to Michael Caine for Best Supporting Actor. Before the Academy Awards ceremony he told reporters, "I'm just going to have a good time, just like when I went in 1970. Then I knew the Academy wouldn't give somebody like me an Oscar, not for *Easy Rider*. So I enjoyed myself. Now? Well, to win would be nice, but so much has gone down in my life that just to be nominated by my peers in the acting community is great. I would accept every year being in this kind of conversation and never winning, honestly."

And after the ceremonies, he expressed no surprise or bitterness at losing. He said, "I felt Michael Caine would win, and he did. I mean, he had been nominated seven times and never had one. I just feel that adds up and ought to be recognized."

Dennis, the former rebel, difficult personality, twice blackballed, was back in the Hollywood fold once more. Celebrated for his acting talents and directing skills, he had accomplished something unique in the annals of Hollywood: a second comeback.

By the time of the following year's Academy Awards, this comeback had put him in the middle of a swirl of controversy once again. Just as *Easy Rider* outraged the "establishment" in the Sixties with its drugged-out counterculture theme, *Colors* proved that Hopper was a rebel for all seasons. When *Colors* opened in April 1988, it was the subject of as many front-page stories as reviews in the entertainment press. Even members of the Los Angeles Police Department who previewed the motion picture turned out to be film critics. One warned that it would "leave dead bodies from one end of this town to the other."

Protests against the film were particularly virulent in L.A. because of the film's depiction of the warfare between Latino and black gangs and the use of actual gang names, Crips and Bloods, and their colors, blue and red, which gang members wear to identify themselves. Protesters marched in front of movie theaters and at Hopper's home in Venice, carrying placards and slogans accusing the film of glorifying gang membership. They tried to lay responsibility for future violence at the feet of Hopper and others involved with the picture's production.

From inside his home, Dennis watched on the closed-circuit video security system as the Guardian Angels, a self-styled community-protection group founded in New York, paraded in front of his home. While they shouted calls to ban *Colors* and taped a picture of Hopper to a toilet seat propped against his front door, Dennis spoke with members of the press in defense of his project: "Blame the killing on the movies? Blame it on kids with guns. Blame it on police who don't have enough guns. Blame it on rock cocaine. Blame it on poverty. But don't blame it on the movies. Films don't kill; people do.

"There's nothing romantic about gangs. None of that *West Side Story* stuff works anymore. What's happening out there, man, it's not romantic at all. There's no glorification of that life in *Colors* at all. *Colors* is about more than gangs. The story is really about an older cop and a younger cop. Boy, if I'd made a story just about the gangs, I'd have never gotten the movie released.

"Yet people who haven't seen the film say it shouldn't be seen. 'Bodies are going to be strewn from one end of this town to the other,' they say. Well, bodies are being strewn from one end of this town to the other now, and while we were making the film it was happening."

Owners of a dozen of the five hundred theaters nationwide scheduled to show it decided against screening *Colors* in the face of the dire predictions of gang warfare. Some theater owners, particularly in the Los Angeles area and to a lesser extent in New York, Chicago, and Miami, beefed up security for the run of the film. Once the movie opened there were a few isolated incidents of violence followed by arrests of suspected gang members at some theaters, but nothing to match the pre-opening predictions that Crips and Bloods would be shooting it out in the aisles.

Most of the shots were directed at the movie by critics. Many praised Hopper's direction, the performances of Duvall and Penn, and the gritty realism enhanced by Haskell Wexler's cinematography. Some reviewers felt that, as a whole, the film tended to be a superficial look at a serious, deep-rooted problem, further burdened with a melodramatic plot concentrating on the cliched conflict between an older cop close to retirement and a hotshot rookie eager to go head to head with the gangbangers. Suspicions were voiced that, without the surrounding controversy, *Colors* would have descended into "B" movie oblivion.

In spite of the protests, or perhaps in part because of them, *Colors* turned out to be a box office success. It did not torpedo Dennis's second career comeback, like *The Last Movie* did the first one.

And this comeback is showing no signs of fading. To be

blackballed by the Hollywood establishment twice, and now to return to the acclaim and the amount of work he had been getting, is remarkable. Dennis's modest assessment of his recent success is: "It's because I'm sober and I'm not taking drugs. I've got really good sobriety and I moved back to Los Angeles and I'm visible and I haven't turned anything down. I'm just taking what's been given to me and I've been very fortunate. The work has been good, the work is good."

He hasn't stopped working since he got truly sober, and that is the way he likes it. At this stage, his work is more important to him than anything else. He has said, "I don't have a personal life." Work is the central focus of his life and what keeps his energy stoked. What he said of himself years before still holds true. He quoted poet Rainer Maria Rilke, saying, "'If it were denied you to create, would you die?'" Having asked that question he went on to say, "If not, then don't create. Do something else. I *have* to create. Otherwise I couldn't justify my insanity."

But now it's the work that keeps the madness at bay. As soon as *Colors* was completed in early 1988, he went into preproduction for another movie, *Backtrack*. He concurs with Warren Beatty, who recently told him, "It's time you play a straight part, someone whose problems are caused by outside forces, not from internal things." *Backtrack* is an erotic thriller which he directs and stars in as a hit man who falls in love with the woman he's been hired to murder.

Besides the current work, he has received overdue recognition for past career achievements. A book of the photographs he took during the 1960s, called *Out of the Sixties*, has been published and fans of his photography as well as his acting come to book signings where he patiently smiles and poses for photographs, often with youngsters who were still in the cradle when he was taking the pictures in the book.

Museums have held retrospectives of Hopper's work. *Dennis Hopper: From Method to Madness* toured the country in 1988 beginning in Minneapolis and going on to New York, Boston, Houston, and Berkeley. The recognition is for Hopper as a complete artist: his painting and photography, as well as his acting and directing.

Dennis doesn't need museum retrospectives to see his past, his present, and his future clearly now. He doesn't regret the experiences, as painful as many of them were, as much as he resents the time and creative potential wasted. He has said, "I was very proud about my drug associations and my dealings and my carrying on in those areas. Very proud of it. And I'm as proud about my sobriety now as I ever was of the other. I'm really having a great time. I have a great time not disorienting my mind.

"A lot of people who were heavier into drugs than me became big stars and continued to work. A lot of them. But I was more honest. My motto in life is, 'Don't tell lies and don't do anything you hate to do.'

"I think it was part of the rebellion against the other culture that wasn't using drugs. We felt free to use them and that was part of our life. But then the people around me straightened up, and I never saw them straightening up. I just got lost in it.

"It's too late to have regrets. It happened. I survived. Most didn't."

INDEX

homes (*cont.*)
West Hollywood, California, 47–48
Hoosiers, 161, 163–165, 166–167,
168, 178, 179
Hopper nominated for Academy
Award for, 178, 179
Hopper nominated for Golden
Globe Award for, 178
Hopper winning honor from
National Society of Film Critics
for, 178
Hopper winning Los Angeles Film
Critics award for, 178
Hopper, Charlotte (sister-in-law), 83,
85
Hopper, David (brother), 5, 7, 16, 34,
83, 85, 102, 103
Hopper, Dennis
adolescence of, 7–29
affair with Archuletta, Ellen, 140,
147, 148
affair with Milinaire, Caterine,
116–117, 122
affair with Thompson, Jaimie, 170
affair with Wood, Natalie, 21, 22,
32, 34–35
in alcohol and drug rehabilitation
facilities, 146–147, 150
alcohol use of, 4, 5, 24, 41, 50, 75,
91, 98, 104, 105, 107, 126, 129,
138, 139, 140, 141, 144, 145,
152–153
appearance of, 23, 38, 73–74, 90,
101, 157, 180
arrests of, 102, 103–104
art of. *See* art
birth of, 2
brother of. *See* Hopper, David
childhood of, 1–6, 24
cigarette smoking of, 24, 105, 147,
183
civil rights movement and, 50–51
cocaine use of, 23–24, 61, 141,
142, 145, 148–149, 151
daughters of. *See* Hopper, Marin;

Hopper, Ruthana
divorces of. *See* Halprin, Daria;
Haywood, Brooke; Phillips,
Michelle
documentary about, 86
dramatic declamation contests won
by, 8
drug use of, 23, 24, 41, 45, 46, 50,
53, 54, 61, 75, 85, 91, 98, 104,
107, 113, 121, 126, 144,
152–153. *See also specific drug*
father of. *See* Hopper, Jay
feelings of emptiness of, 97, 98,
100, 108, 149
fiftieth birthday of, 172–173
gasoline sniffing by, as child, 4, 24
grandparents of, maternal, 2, 3, 4,
5
guns and, 53, 102, 103, 104, 111,
126, 140
hallucinations of, 107, 108, 140,
145–146, 147, 149–150
heroin used by, 105, 142–143
Hollywood blackballing of, 38, 96,
106, 110, 111, 189
hospitalization of, psychiatric, 150
imagination of, as child, 1, 2, 3,
5–6, 7
job of, first, 10
job of, first theater, 11, 12
karate and, 53, 54
lack of interest in school of, 6, 8
LSD used by, 62, 83
marijuana legalization advocated
by, 104
marijuana used by, 8, 19–20, 24,
74, 81, 105, 126, 139
marriages of. *See* Halprin, Daria;
Hayword, Brooke; Phillips,
Michelle
mental breakdowns of, 144–147,
149–151
mother of. *See* Hopper, Marjorie
Davis
mysticism and, 106–107